AF255729

Test All Things

Test All Things

The Bible, Faith, and Science

Gijsbert van den Brink

CASCADE *Books* · Eugene, Oregon

TEST ALL THINGS
The Bible, Faith, and Science

Cascade Books
An Imprint of Wipf and Stock Publishers
199 W. 8th Ave., Suite 3
Eugene, OR 97401

www.wipfandstock.com

PAPERBACK ISBN: 978-1-6667-6156-6
HARDCOVER ISBN: 978-1-6667-6157-3
EBOOK ISBN: 978-1-6667-6158-0

Cataloguing-in-Publication data:

Names: Van den Brink, Gijsbert, author.

Title: Test all things : the Bible, faith, and science / Gijsbert van den Brink.

Description: Eugene, OR: Cascade Books, 2023 | Includes bibliographical references and index.

Identifiers: ISBN 978-1-6667-6156-6 (paperback) | ISBN 978-1-6667-6157-3 (hardcover) | ISBN 978-1-6667-6158-0 (ebook)

Subjects: LCSH: Science and theology. | Religion and science—History. | Bible.

Classification: BL240.2 V295 2023 (print) | BL240 (ebook)

07/14/23

Translation by Harry Cook

Originally published in Dutch as *Onderzoek alle dingen* by KokBoekencentrum, Utrecht © 2021.

Contents

Introduction

Few developments have changed our daily lives in recent centuries as radically as the rise of modern science. We hardly realize how different life was when we didn't yet deal with the many applications of scientific research. I still remember how one of the professors with whom I took classes pointed us to the *faucet;* most people nowadays have quite a number of them in their homes. We usually open them without a further thought. In fact, we rarely think about how strange it really is that we take them for granted. But during most of human history, and still in many places in the world today, the water supply is, of course, an extraordinarily complex business. Not only obtaining water, but also purifying and distributing it, were daunting tasks: complex, dangerous, and certainly time-consuming. Whether you had to go to the pump in the village or to a nearby river, so that you could carry water back to your house, getting clean water was always a big undertaking.

You don't normally think of faucets as one of the great achievements of modern technology, and I think that is why my professor used them as an example. There is, of course, a lot of know-how and organization behind the faucets that we open every day: a whole network of water pipes, sewers, water treatment plants, etc. Even such an old phenomenon as faucets still has a huge impact on our everyday lives, let alone all kinds of later technological developments that are the result of scientific research. Our lives have truly changed unrecognizably from that of someone living in, say, the sixteenth century. For this reason, it is always an interesting thought experiment to imagine how a person from the past that you admire—say someone like John Calvin or, perhaps, your own great-grandfather or great-grandmother—would react if they could be moved into our world with a time machine. Undoubtedly they would be totally amazed by everything that they would see and experience. It would probably take some time before they would even understand how our lives work. Unfortunately, we will never know what they would really think and what they would say to us about it. Possibly, however, after they would have thought about it for a time, they would point out that even though much has changed, human beings themselves have remained the same.

The World of Science and the Bible

The enormous changes that have come with the rise of science and of what we call the "scientific worldview" have also had consequences for the way we experience our faith. Honesty compels us to recognize that these developments have caused the Bible to take a more distant place, in many ways, in our lives. To use a concise word that one often finds in the literature, our world has become *disenchanted.* We look everywhere for causal connections, for cause-and-effect relationships, and we no longer think in terms of spirits or gods that work behind the scenes to influence events. What does that mean for the faith in the God of Israel, the Father of the Lord Jesus Christ? And how can the Bible still speak authoritatively to us in a time that is marked by our technological achievements? Those are important questions. But we also reverse our perspective: how does the Bible shape our view of the exalted and dominant place that contemporary science and technology have now taken? How can the Bible help us to get a sharper view of their limitations and risks? These are some of the questions that we want to explore through a series of Bible studies about faith and the sciences.

In these explorations, the Bible is our point of departure. We view the Bible as the Word of God, through which God speaks to us humans and shows us the way, also today. At the same time, we realize that the Bible is also a book that was written by people a long time ago but not unlike us. They were inspired by God's Spirit, but, as we shall see, they were not necessarily separated from their own personal, cultural, and historical backgrounds. In numerous places in the Bible we obviously find the traces of those backgrounds. Over the past couple of centuries, theological and historical research has opened our eyes to this. In the Bible studies that follow we will see how taking such research seriously can help us to understand what is going on in the texts to be discussed and how that illuminates our own situation.

In brief, we take as our starting point what theologians like Abraham Kuyper and Herman Bavinck have called the organic theory (or doctrine) of inspiration: the Spirit has moved people to write texts that would later form the Bible, but has employed them with all their human qualities, as the people that they were—so in an organic way. This double nature of the Bible—Word of God and human word at the same time—is often experienced as rather problematic. That may be the case because we are a bit too eager to know exactly what is the relationship between these two. However, it is better to see the beauty, and even the uniqueness of the Bible in these two aspects. Apparently, that is how God wanted it to be. It is precisely through this colorful collection of human writings, handed down in shreds of papyrus and rolls of parchment, that God wants to address us, guide us, help us, and, especially, wants us to get to know him. It is with grateful expectation that we can turn to the Bible, time and again.

The Complex Relationship between Science and Faith

In the Bible studies that follow, we will focus on the relationship between faith and science—meaning by science not just the natural sciences, but academic scholarship more generally conceived. We know from history that this relationship is very complex. At times both were diametrically opposed to each other. But most of the time it just seemed that way and many other issues played a role in the background. That was the case, for example, in the infamous "Galileo affair"—which has become iconic as the conflict par excellence between scientific insight and coercion by communities of faith. Historians have been able to discern much more precisely what actually happened in the Galileo case and, as a result, have drastically adjusted this picture. The case turned out to be much more complex than Galileo's science simply coming into conflict with the faith of his church at the time. Numerous other issues—among which was Galileo's difficult character—also played a role. In any case, this does not appear to have been a conflict between faith and science, if for no other reason than Galileo's giving a religious explanation to his findings. On the other hand, you cannot say that the relationship between faith and science has always been very harmonious. There have definitely been tensions and conflicts, and some of these still occur today.

Sometimes you also encounter the idea that faith and science have nothing to do with each other. They would be two entities (languages or even worlds) that are entirely separate from each other. This thought can give the impression of the highly educated expert who knows so much better than the ordinary masses who are always so worried about this relationship without realizing that there really is nothing to worry about here. At the same time, authors who suggest there is such an independence between faith and science write long treatises on their relationship. It is indeed puzzling how some people manage to write whole books about two things that, they say, have nothing to do with each other. In the Bible studies that follow we shall assume that faith and science do touch each other, and will therefore always alternate exegetical explorations of Scripture passages and relevant scientific or historical information. In this it will indeed become clear that the two are not separate from each other, but rather can illuminate each other and be related to each other in intriguing ways.

In this book we pay special attention to the topic that today is regarded as the foremost area of conflict in the relationship between faith and science: the question of whether the biological theory of evolution as developed by Charles Darwin and further elaborated by other biologists is compatible with biblical faith. Opinions about this are still divided—among Christians as well as among Jews, Muslims, and atheists. In 2020, I wrote a separate book about the question of whether Christian faith and neo-Darwinian evolution are compatible (*Reformed Theology and Evolutionary Theory*, Eerdmans). Some readers of the book found it regrettable that whereas I went into theological topics in detail, I did not (apart from the well-known chapters, Genesis 1–3) separately discuss various Bible texts that are also relevant to the topic. For this reason I now want to offer a reading of various relevant biblical passages (particularly in chapters 4–7). If we assume that the theory of evolution is more or less correct, is it still possible to give a convincing interpretation of important Bible passages that seem to point in a different direction, or does that lead to contrived explanations? Can the Bible itself shed light, perhaps, on the purpose and meaning of the evolutionary history? Even if we in these Bible studies explore the various possibilities that present themselves, we are not concerned with forcing a particular answer to these questions—the readers may think for themselves! That is also why conversation questions have been added to each chapter, to enable you as a reader to consider things further, either in a group or for yourself.

How to Use This Book

I do hope that this book will be helpful, both for people who want to deepen their personal faith or want to know how their faith relates to science, as well as for people who use it for a guide in discussion groups. I am thinking of church discussion groups or student groups at colleges or universities. Particularly as a student, I imagine, one regularly encounters questions about the relationship between the Bible, faith, and scientific scholarship. In the Bible studies presented here, this relationship is discussed not only in a general sense but also where it concerns many concrete scientific fields—so I use "scientific" in a very broad sense here: physics, astronomy, cosmology, biology, psychology, history, climate science, literary studies, philosophy, and, of course, biblical studies and theology. Thus, you can have extensive discussions about exciting questions that arise from your own field of study. You can also participate in such discussions if you are not a student or are no longer a student and are interested in these kinds of questions. The number of Bible studies, ten in all, can be covered in one or two seasons. The scope and profundity of these Bible studies may be a little more extensive than what is customary, but the aim is to really deepen your understanding of the topics covered. In all this, I have tried to avoid jargon and to write as clearly as possible.

The New Revised Standard Version (NRSV) of the Bible has been used as the basis of these studies. The NRSV lends itself well for study purposes because of its text fidelity ("formal equivalence"). The New International Version, which is more oriented to the target language ("dynamic equivalence"), or other translations, can also contribute to your discussions. In group discussions it is always helpful to have several translations available, in print or digitally, so that you can hear how these various translations are rendering the text that is being discussed. The conversation questions at the end of the chapters aim to not be too confining, but are intended to be helpful to come to a good and meaningful discussion about the topics at hand. This also applies to the group activity that is suggested at the end of every chapter. Needless to say, the book can also perfectly be used for personal reading.

Amsterdam, June 2023
Gijsbert van den Brink

Acknowledgments

As mentioned, the New Revised Standard Version (NRSV, © 1989) has been used for all Scripture references unless otherwise indicated.

Figure 1 in chapter 2 has been adapted, with permission, from an illustration by Scott Buchanan.

The story of the chaplain and the biology professor in chapter 4 is by Dr. Michael R. Wagenman ("Are Ancient Bible Stories Still Relevant?" © *The Banner* (July/Aug 2020). Reprinted with permission. All rights reserved worldwide).

I thank my colleague, Dr. Rik Peels (VU Amsterdam) for his feedback on an earlier version of the text, Rev. Bob DeMoor for reading the book and making many helpful suggestions, and, of course, Professor Harry Cook (The King's University, Edmonton) both for his many stimulating comments and for his wonderful translation of the Dutch precursor of this book.

Finally, this publication was made possible through the support of a grant from Templeton World Charity Foundation. The opinions expressed in this publication are those of the author and do not necessarily reflect the views of Templeton World Charity Foundation.

1

Wisdom and Science

Science as it is practiced today did not yet exist at the time the Bible was written. So we can't go to the Bible to ask "how God thinks about science." Nevertheless, indirectly, the Bible has all kinds of things to say that are important for our evaluation and practice of science, and also about the relationship between science and faith. In this chapter we're starting to look at that. For while we may not find much about science in the Bible, it does frequently deal with wisdom. And also with knowledge, for that matter—and with insight, formation, perceptiveness, and the willingness to listen. How are these concepts related to each other, and to what we call "science" today? And what do they mean theologically, that is, in light of God's relationship with us? To begin, we will investigate this on the basis of the opening verses of Proverbs. We'll see that there certainly is similarity between science (and scholarly knowledge in general) and wisdom—but there are also differences.

Read: Proverbs 1:1–7

Wisdom—Word by Word

We decided to make our start by stepping over the threshold of the book of Proverbs, and as we do so, we enter a unique world of words. Not unlike entering a cathedral for the first time, we have to orient ourselves, and take a look around—where have we ended up precisely? The opening passage helps us to get an eye for the most important connections. When we list the key concepts in the King James Version and the New Revised Standard Version and add some other translation options, it looks like this:

	KJV	NRSV	Also possible
2	wisdom	wisdom	art of living
	instruction	instruction	criticism, correction
	understanding	insight	discernment
3	justice	righteousness	moral integrity
	judgment	justice	honesty
	equity	equity	impartiality
4	subtlety	shrewdness	thoughtfulness
	knowledge	knowledge	understanding
	discretion	prudence	perceptiveness
5	wise counsel	learning, skill	deliberation
6	interpretation	figure	explanation
	dark sayings	riddles	hidden meanings
7	fear of the Lord	fear of the Lord	respect for God
	beginning	beginning	principle, nucleus, foundation

Besides these key words, it is also important to pay attention to the verbs, especially those verbs in the passage that are preceded by "to" and that describe the purpose of the book of Proverbs. In the KJV those verbs are: to know, perceive, receive, hear, increase, attain, and then, once again, understand. They are all words that indicate what the wise person concentrates on. In contrast, only one word is used as typical for fools: despise. The foolish person is apparently characterized by an indifferent, contemptuous attitude.

It is good to let all these words sink in for a moment, without necessarily worrying about how they all hang together. How do they sound? And how do they touch our own lives? I first wrote these sentences during the time in which the coronavirus pandemic was having its dire effects. Every day the statistics of hospitalizations and deaths were reported, and while vaccines became available, no one knew how the pandemic was going to end. In any case, it suddenly became clear that we have a great need for *wise* people. For kings, that is to say, for government leaders who, like Solomon, could show us the ways that we should go. For that we needed precisely the qualities that we see listed here: wisdom, insight, willingness to be corrected, discernment, reason, thoughtfulness, and wisdom. Numerous human lives depend on whether leaders are gifted with these qualities. And indeed, we see how heads of government who would be labeled by the book of Proverbs as "foolish" make countless victims due to mismanagement and horrendous decisions that ruin lives.

Are wisdom, insight, willingness to listen, and so on, qualities that you either have or don't have, without being able to do much about it? It is striking that according to the Proverbs passage you are apparently not born with them. For you have to *search* for them. In fact, we are constantly called upon to do so. Apparently, we can set ourselves to *grow* in wisdom. In this there is a surprising paradox: it is precisely those who are already wise who will make this their inclination (v. 5). Thus, there is wisdom present in the desire to *become* wise and sensible. The ancient philosophers said it already: real wisdom consists of a desire for wisdom, that is, *philo-sophia*. In short, this is not about the IQ that you received but about your attitude. According to the poet who wrote Proverbs, this attitude is born out of respect for God: the "fear of the LORD." This respect is the origin of knowledge. So apparently those who are in communion with God are interested in knowledge, in wisdom, and in the continuous increase in insight and discernment. King Solomon, who is credited with these words, excelled in these qualities, as is clear from what is told about him in 1 Kings 3.

Wisdom: A Description

The word "wisdom" is generally a somewhat vague and dated concept. However, what is meant by it is immediately clarified when the author puts all those other concepts alongside it. They add color to the picture, so to speak, so that it becomes increasingly more concrete. Wisdom, oddly enough perhaps, has first of all to do with "correction"—that is, with the ability to accept criticism. Thus, the wise person listens to what other people say. In particular, he or she listens to people who know things better than they do. A special mention is given to teachers (vv. 5, 6) and also parents (v. 8). But precisely in between, in the heart of it (v. 7), the author points to the Lord God. Therefore, as needed, the wise person lets themselves be corrected and disciplined by God and people. In this sense, wise people are the opposite of stubborn people who think they have a monopoly on wisdom. Wise people realize how much they are indebted to others, even to those who are critical of them.

In addition, wisdom is accompanied by insight and discernment. In the tangle of opinions and facts, you have to know what really matters. Above all, the ability to discern relates to good and evil. With no less than three words—justice, judgement, and equity (KJV)—it is pointed out that wisdom has an important moral component. This is why being wise is something different from being clever. Even though you also need discernment for cleverness, you can nevertheless use that ability for your own goals, and those can be very selfish goals. Then you will be found to be clever, even cunning. Wisdom, on the other hand, focuses precisely on what is good in an objective sense, on integrity, and on what is morally just. For this reason, there is a strong connection in the Jewish religion between wisdom and the Torah. After all, in the first five books of the Bible, we are taught what is good and just; the commandments and promises of the Lord point this out concretely.

What wisdom includes is made more concrete with words such as astuteness, understanding, and reflection. These words stress the importance of considering things before you shout, say, or do anything. Of course, one person can do this more readily than another—not all people are equally quick to understand. But that is not the point here. It's important here to not just go by your intuitions that spontaneously impose themselves on you, because these are often prematurely formed judgements—or prejudices. Although intuitions can be correct, they should be judged by considering them critically before basing your actions on them. The sensible person considers things as much as possible in order to discover his or her personal biases. That person proceeds with caution and consultation and, according to the Proverbs poet, is also characterized by what I have described above as *perceptiveness*. You are perceptive when you play close attention to what is going on around you, when you manage to even pick up small signals. This requires you to not be too introverted or busy in your own world; instead, you can attempt to be really open to the world around you. For young people who are still unpracticed at this (called the "simple" here), it is important to learn this skill (v. 4). But even those who have come to understanding do well to continue to focus on this. After all, you also have to increase and deepen your insight in a lifelong process of continuous self-education. Indeed, the poet who wrote Proverbs is clearly a proponent of what today is called continuing education. In this way you not only gather wisdom and insight, but also just plain *knowledge*.

Knowledge and Science

Now it is often said that the knowledge spoken of here is a different knowledge than the knowledge that contemporary science strives for. And it is indeed good not to equate the two. Philosophers distinguish between intellectual knowledge on the one hand and on the other what can be designated as experiential knowledge based on familiarity and acquaintance. Intellectual knowledge can be expressed in all kinds of claims and in statements that you make (in "propositions" the philosophers say)—claims that you can then try to "prove." Experiential knowledge cannot always be translated into concrete statements and usually cannot be proven. It can only be acquired in personal experiences, and especially in encounters that you have with someone. That is why it is sometimes described as relational knowledge. The Bible often deals with this kind of knowledge: Knowledge that comes along with personal contacts, with love, and with a sense of wonder. Here, in Proverbs 1, this type of knowledge is acknowledged when it tells us that *reverence* for God is the major part of knowledge.

Nevertheless, it is not good to totally separate these two types of knowledge and, as is often done, to contrast them as if they were completely different from each other. The Hebrew word that is used for "knowledge" is a very common word that refers to knowledge in general, both practical and more theoretical. A comment in one of my Dutch Bibles about the word in verse 4 suggests, aptly: "understand with this that it includes not only the simple knowledge of facts but also the underlying connections." So, it's also about understanding and insight. Interestingly, the same Bible translation (the Dutch equivalent of the KJV, dated 1637) renders the Hebrew word for knowledge in verses 4 and 7 as "wetenschap"—which is currently the Dutch word for all forms of science and scholarship. Back then "wetenschap" did not refer to the sciences (and all scholarly disciplines) as we know them today; after all, science only came into being during the course of the seventeenth century. At the time, the word referred to everything there is to know, that is, knowledge in general.

Yet, in what we call science today, in the wide sense of scholarly research, the acquisition of such knowledge-in-general is also important, especially in the sense of insight in underlying connections. So there is no clear-cut division between science and everyday knowledge. It is striking how many of the characteristics mentioned in the right row of the chart above are totally essential for the practice of scholarly investigations, and are fully applied there. This begins with "correction" that needs to be accepted—that is, with openness to criticism. In particular since the work of the Austrian-British philosopher of science, Karl Popper (1902–1994), it has become clear how incredibly important it is for scientists to expose their theories to criticism, and on the basis of that criticism, to adjust or even abandon these theories. Scholars are accustomed to presenting the articles they write to at least two or three, but sometimes ten or twenty, colleagues so they can make their articles stronger by incorporating the feedback they have received. (An aside: one wonders if the sermons of preachers wouldn't become more effective if they would follow the same practice from time to time.)

But other qualities and attitudes mentioned by the author of Proverbs in the opening passage are also of great importance in the natural and social sciences. This applies, for example, to discernment. Perhaps the core of what scientists do is to distinguish well: to consistently apply the same distinctions and divisions. To this we add perceptiveness: as a professional scholar you have to know well what to look for, and that cannot always be formulated precisely. This applies to the natural scientist as well as the historian, the linguist, and the physician. For example, it takes practice for medical students who want to listen to fetal heart sounds in a pregnant woman to distinguish these from background noise. Of course, they have been told what kinds of sound they must listen for, but there are so many other sounds (for example the heartbeat of the pregnant mother) that it takes a lot of attention and careful observation to be able to distinguish them.

Scholarly Virtues

Scientists must be creative and think for themselves, of course. But oddly enough, perhaps, their thinking nevertheless begins with them simply accepting many things their teachers have told them—including some things that they will come to understand gradually as they go along. Thus, importantly, they must hear (v. 4), that is, be prepared to listen. Those who cross the line from creativity to stubbornness will, eventually, not be taken seriously—and usually rightly so; it is seldom that the passed-on knowledge turns out to be wrong.

Furthermore, honesty (v. 3) is also an extremely important value in science. Nowadays, this is usually referred to as "integrity." Speaking about my own context: every PhD doctoral student who works at a Dutch university must sign the code of conduct for scientific integrity: you must promise that you have played the game fairly, have not manipulated the data, have worked transparently and carefully, have not appropriated the findings of others, and so on. If you cross the line here as a scientist, it can bring a lot of misery your way. Such cases connected with the name of initially renowned scholars are well known.

Scholarly integrity also includes—and there are many transgressions here—that you, as a scientist, do not speak on matters beyond your expertise. It is a regrettable matter when, for example, natural or social scientists make all kinds of pronouncements about morals or the existence of God, and in doing so suggest that they make these statements *as scientists.* In doing so, they give their statements a significance that they do not deserve. In the same way, theologians should, of course, be wary of making statements that extend beyond the boundaries of their field. Proverbs 1, as we saw, mentions other virtues that come with wisdom, such as prudence, consultation, and thoughtfulness. Scientists should excel in these too. They should therefore not be guided by prejudices or entrenched ways of thinking.

How difficult the latter can be was demonstrated in the first wave of the coronavirus epidemic. Hardly anyone dared to draw the necessary difficult conclusions from the facts that were already known. We simply couldn't imagine that things would become as serious as they did, and that our lives would be turned upside down. Even dyed-in-the-wool scientists supported the idea of easier solutions (such as the quick development of "group immunity"). For too long there was a mentality of "it's not going to be too bad" and "we can obviously handle this." Only a few, such as the well-known Dutch virologist Ab Osterhaus, put the hard scientific facts first. From there he dared to take the role of prophet of doom upon himself by insisting upon drastic and incisive measures from the outset. Only when scientists focus on gaining insight in these ways will they be able to come up with good explanations, with in-depth interpretations (v. 6) that will extend our knowledge. All good scholarship in all its branches—the natural and social sciences and the humanities—depends on such explanations and clarifications. So, there's a lot of wisdom needed in this regard.

But, of course, that's also the case outside the world of scholarship! Also in everyday life, the virtues we mentioned are of outstanding importance and it is important to make them part of our lives. Good scientists are often (though certainly not always) wise people. Fortunately, however, wisdom is more than science: it can also be found in other areas of life. There, too, you have people who can accept criticism, act thoughtfully, have discernment, radiate the art of living, and so on. You don't have to have an extensive education to be familiar with these aspects of wisdom. Numerous academically trained pastors have, throughout the centuries, recounted how much they learned in their first and later congregations from a wise elder who certainly did not have a university education but had much life experience and a great ability in dealing with people. Such elders often excelled (and excel) in what we named experiential knowledge above: knowledge that arises from the concrete interactions with people and from the careful observation of all kinds of processes that occur between people, and between humanity and nature. That kind of practical knowledge helps you not only to understand matters, but also to withstand with grace all the situations that life presents. Hence the word *wisdom* that is used in Proverbs 1 can also be translated as "the art of living."

Respect for God as the Source of Knowledge

It is remarkable that in the book of Proverbs we are presented with many wisdoms that were also known in other parts of the ancient Eastern world. For example, quite a few biblical proverbs are literally found in Egyptian wisdom books. It is somewhat far-fetched to assume that these were by definition later texts that were influenced by the biblical Proverbs. In fact, the reverse is also conceivable. In any case, there were at the time high-level international relations in which wisdom literature was also exchanged. In this connection, think of the visit made by the Queen of Sheba to Solomon (1 Kgs 10:1–13; 2 Chr 9:1–12). Many recommendations and instructions in Proverbs therefore have a general human character. They are not aimed specifically at the people of Israel, but at everyone. Often they do not exhort us to believe in God, but rather to use common sense and to be mindful of discipline.

It is all the more remarkable, therefore, that in the climax of the opening passage, respect for YHWH, the God of Israel, is emphatically given a central place. Possibly, Solomon or a later editor intentionally added this accent to connect the general human wisdoms that were around with the faith in Israel's God. In other places in Proverbs too, the importance of our commitment to God and his work are pointed out. This is done for the first time here when it is said, "Reverence for the LORD is the seed of knowledge." Or in the classical formulation, "The fear of the LORD is the beginning of wisdom" (see also Ps 111:10, Prov 9:10, and Job 28:28). The statement is the cornerstone, literally and figuratively, of many Christian schools.

How exactly should we understand this sentence? While the expression is familiar, answering this question with certainty is more difficult. But when we interpret the text from its context, the following picture emerges. The person who fears God has reverence for him. That means that he or she always takes God into account. You will not go on to all kinds of opinions of your own about what is good and true, but you orient yourself to God to learn from him. You do not want to twist the will of God or manipulate it toward your own views; instead, you want to serve God in ways that he wants. That's why you listen to God's voice as attentively as you can. Thus, the wise person attentively studies how God has made himself known, and organizes his or her life accordingly (Ps 1). For that person has an enormous respect for God. And because the wise make that "de-centering" movement, so that they themselves are not the center of meaning but look beyond themselves for what is to be the center of their lives, they learn to know God. In this way, the reverent focus on God leads to deeper understanding of who God is and what he wants.

Now the text does not only say that reverence for God leads to a deeper knowledge *of God*. It states that reverence for God is the source or principle of knowledge in general. We may understand this in such a way that whoever has this reverence of God will also want to adopt a similar attitude towards God's creation. So, you are going to take an open stance toward both people and things; you want to know them really well, and understand their behavior. And you don't impose your own ideas and thinking schemes on the outside world (whether that be people or natural phenomena) but you let that outside world speak for itself, so to say. You do not project your own ideas upon reality but you seek to understand the language that this reality speaks. It is too simplistic to suggest that contemporary science is a direct result of this attitude. Historically speaking, it's a little more complicated than that. Yet, according to historians of science, Christianity at the time of the Reformation did give a huge boost to the emergence of science because Christians started to read nature as literally as they had started to read the Bible: searching for what nature itself says, even if it sometimes goes against what we ourselves wish or think. Thus, people started to marvel at the distinctiveness of nature, and began to see it as "a beautiful book in which all creatures, great and small, are as letters to make us ponder the invisible things of God," such as God's power and divinity (Belgic Confession, art. 2; see Rom 1:20). Thus, reverence for God became a source of knowledge—and it remains such a source today.

Discussion Questions

1. The book of Proverbs is often not as highly regarded as some other books in the Bible. It is less popular than Job, Ecclesiastes, and the Song of Solomon, and, certainly, than the Psalms or the Gospels. Talk about why that is. And also talk about the extent to which that is justified.

2. Both believers and nonbelievers often put the Bible and science over against each other, as if they were fire and water. Why would that be? Can Proverbs 1 help us adjust that image?

3. Modern science has, in important ways, significant Judeo-Christian roots. Nevertheless, a significant percentage of scientists today are not religious. Is that because contemporary science facilitates disbelief? Or do you see other causes?

4. What does it tell you that reverence for God is the core and foundation of knowledge?

Group Activity

Divide those present into two groups. One group collects examples and arguments that show that faith and science are often in conflict with each other, to the detriment of each other. The other group collects supporting materials for the proposition that faith and science are in beautiful harmony and can strengthen each other. It doesn't matter what you yourself think; participate in your group. After some time, talk about which arguments or examples impressed you the most. How would you, all things considered, characterize the relationship between faith and science?

2

World Pictures in the Bible

THROUGHOUT ALL TIMES, PEOPLE have formed for themselves an image of the world in which they live, and how it is put together. That was also the case in the Middle East at the time the various books of the Bible were written. We can call such an image a world picture. We see hints of the world picture of the time in various places in the Bible. In this chapter we will examine this topic somewhat more closely on the basis of a special passage: the text of the Ten Commandments. In this, we do not focus directly on the intent of these commandments for us today, but we pay attention to how the world picture of the first hearers and readers plays a role in the background. Surprisingly, we shall see that the way this world picture in the Bible shows through does not, in any way, detract from the enduring expressive power of the texts in question.

Read: Exodus 20:1–17

World Picture in a Broader Sense

Our current world picture is, in its main features, still determined by the work of the Polish astronomer Nicolaus Copernicus (1473–1543). According to Copernicus, the sun does not move around the Earth, as everyone thought at that time, but the exact opposite is the case: the Earth, like all other planets, moves in a fixed orbit around the sun. Later, our world picture was expanded greatly, of course. Our solar system turned out to be not the only one, but one of many, in an almost immeasurable universe. The vast distances within the universe can bewilder us. The sun, too, turned out to not be the center, but only a miniscule pinhead somewhere in a inconspicuous part of the universe. But we may still see in all of this the work of "God, the Father almighty, creator of heaven and earth." And we may believe that God will not abandon his creation; this faith and trust is apparently independent of the particular world picture that we hold.

In Exodus 20 we very clearly see indications of life as it was lived in Israel at that time. People lived in a largely agrarian society; hence we see references in the fourth and tenth commandments to cattle kept, to domestic servants employed or kept as slaves, and in the fifth commandment to the crucial importance of good relationships between parents and children (v. 12). It also becomes clear how the male-female relationship was seen at the time: the woman was regarded as the property of the man. It is remarkable that, when it comes to wrongful desires, even the house of the (male) neighbor is mentioned first, and then, subsequently, his wife. For us, today, that is difficult to swallow. After this, the neighbor's male and female slave are mentioned, and then his other possessions.

In Deuteronomy 5 we encounter a slightly revised version of the Ten Commandments; here the wife is mentioned first, and then the other possible objects of desire follow. But in both versions of the text the world picture of the time shows itself between the lines. That can be painful, for example, for women who have experienced firsthand the negative consequences of patriarchal thinking. Nevertheless, we are usually able to distinguish the cultural settings from their actual intent. In the tenth commandment, it is simply about not casting a desirous eye upon something that belongs to someone else. Starting with this intent it is not difficult to think of other variants of the commandment that are applicable to our time ("You shall not cast a jealous eye on the Tesla of your neighbor"). These do not change the meaning of the commandment but translate it, as it were, into our contemporary world picture and situation.

World Pictures in a More Restricted Sense

In the previous section we dealt with what we might call the "world picture" in a broad sense: the sum of historically and culturally determined images and customs that are current at a particular time. In what follows now, however, we want to focus specifically on the "world picture" in a more restricted sense. By this we mean the picture that people have in their minds when they think of the world with everything that goes with it. Consciously or not, everyone has kind of an image of how the world and the whole of the cosmos are put together. That is also the case in the Bible.

That is not to say that there is one well-defined world picture in the Bible. For this, the time frame of the many hundreds of years in which the Bible came into being is too great: in such a long time, aspects of how one looks at the world inevitably shift. In addition, we must realize that particularly in the Old Testament, often more or less separate traditions have been brought together. All these traditions bore witness to the same God, even though the local or regional backgrounds might differ. Sometimes very different names were used for God.

The texts that have been brought together in the so-called historical books of the Old Testament have a fascinating origin that is as complex as it is interesting. Thus, it is not surprising that we encounter traces of different world pictures in the Bible. One time the earth is on pillars (Job 9:6) or foundations (Ps 104:5); another time it is founded on the seas (Ps 24:2). One time it has four corners (Rev 7:1, 20:8); another time God is enthroned above "the circle of the earth" (Isa 40:22). Even heaven can have four corners (Jer 49:36) or stand on pillars (Job 26:11). It is conceivable, of course, that these expressions are symbolically intended, especially in poetic writings such as Job or the Psalms. But then, too, they usually derive from what was "really believed" at an earlier stage. Symbolic expressions also come from somewhere.

Thus the world picture in the ancient Middle East was not always and everywhere the same. So it is understandable that the way the various Bible authors looked at the structure of the cosmos was not the same across the board. In general, people didn't think as systematically as we do now. People then were much more concerned with the powers that could be exerted by the various celestial bodies, or by water, and they saw these elements as mobile. Our modern world picture is, as we saw, "disenchanted." It has become businesslike: you can deal with things in a manageable, clear approach. It also makes a tight distinction between living beings and inanimate things. In the experience of the Eastern person these were not so clearly divided. Their world picture was more ambiguous, dynamic, and unpredictable. Danger could threaten from anywhere. You could be attacked from every side by demonic powers that employed the elements. Therefore, you would do well to keep on the good side of those elements by paying them the necessary respect. Hence, a heavenly body like the sun was often honored like a deity.

For the Israelite, however, God's revelation showed decisively that God is above all these forces of nature. So much so that they were barely allowed to have a name. As we will see in chapter 5, for example, the sun in Genesis 1 is just a big ball of light. You certainly shouldn't bow down to it! Even the waters under the earth are hardly threatening. God stands above them all. He made everything and maintains everything. The mountains and trees cheer for him too (Isa 55:12). In this way, world pictures of the time are brought under his dominion.

The Tiered World Picture of the Ancient Middle East

Thus, we can't just talk about "the world picture of the Bible," or even of the Old Testament. There's too much variation for that. Nevertheless, at the same time it is remarkable how much *similarity* there is between the world pictures that we encounter here and there between the lines of the Old Testament. These in turn correspond at times with the New Testament and even more clearly with other sources from the Near East (particularly from ancient Mesopotamia). In this way, researchers have been able to reconstruct some outlines of the "ancient Near Eastern world picture" that can be perceived in the Bible. This is the so-called "three-layered" world picture, a very simple image of which is depicted in Figure 1.

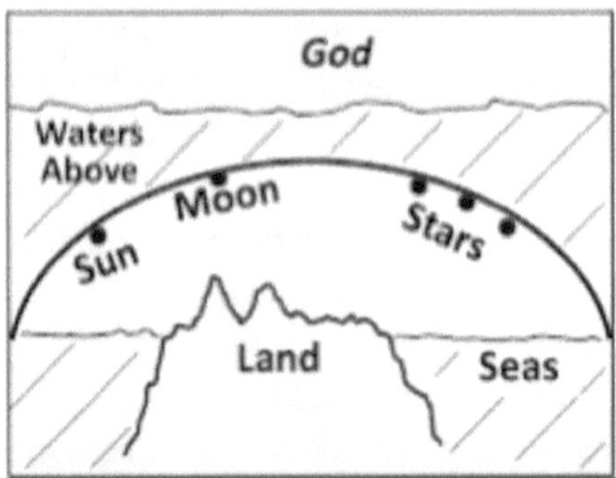

Fig. 1. Ancient Near Eastern view of the world.

Once we have this picture in mind, we understand how we must comprehend Exodus 20:4. For here the Israelites were forbidden to make an image of "anything that is in heaven above" (such as the sun, moon, and stars—heavenly bodies that were often depicted and honored as gods in Egypt), of anything "that is on the earth beneath," but also that is "in the water under the earth" (such as fishes). These are exactly the three layers that exist in this ancient Eastern world picture (as shown in Figure 1). Sometimes it is argued that the Israelites could not see the waters beneath the earth and that it would be strange, therefore, to ban the worship of animals that exist there. But as the picture shows, the waters under the earth could indeed be seen from the edges of the earth, as the easterner imagined it to be. Even if that were not the case, one could well imagine the monsters that were supposed to be swimming there (Ps 148:7; Ps 104:25) and be tempted to worship them out of fear. Thus, in Deuteronomy 4:18, the people of Israel were explicitly forbidden to make an image "of any fish that is in the water under the earth." The same applies to any heavenly bodies that are above the earth.

We also find this three-tiered world picture in the New Testament, for example in Philippians 2. This text does not deal with animals or things that one would like to worship, but with people that are present in heaven, on earth, or in the underworld (beneath the earth). All those people, Paul writes, shall bend the knee at the name of Jesus (v. 10). Incidentally, it's not entirely certain to what extent Paul did indeed imagine reality as three-layered (although that would not be strange given the influence of the Old Testament on his thinking). It's also possible that in Philippians 2 Paul uses a fixed expression, a saying derived from the former world picture. Just as we can also say, for example, that someone "moved heaven and earth" to get something done, when we now know that the universe consists of many celestial bodies. We simply mean then that that person has done everything possible to get something done. Similarly, Paul means that in the future, all things and all people will bow down to Jesus.

Meaning and Significance

Once we see that the second commandment's formulation is shaped by this ancient Near Eastern world picture, we discover the actual meaning of a text like Exodus 20:4. We conclude that we should not be distracted by this world picture, as if it were authoritative for Christians today. After all, it is not a question of us adopting this world picture that is in the background here for we now know that reality is structured differently from what is depicted here. But that does not matter, because the *significance* of what is said is still crystal clear. Short and to the point: do not make an idol out of anything!

In the theory of interpretation (or hermeneutics) a distinction is sometimes made between the *meaning* and the *significance* of a statement or text. The meaning of Exodus 20:4 can be described in terms of the world picture at the time. But the significance greatly exceeds that. It is still very understandable even though we have a completely different world picture today. After all, God forbids us here to make an image of any creature in order to worship it and so keep on the good side of it—no matter where in the cosmos that creature is found. When we consider how strongly the Eastern person of that time would feel attracted to the unpredictable power of celestial bodies and other forces of nature, we realize how much this second commandment was relevant to the thought of that day. We even come to understand how relevant the commandment still is, given the attraction that astrology and other forms of divinizing natural phenomena exert even today. That attraction is often accompanied by fear—a fear that, in turn, can lead to slavish worship and subservient behavior. The God of Israel wants to shield his people from all that. After all, he has freed his people for a reason.

How do we do justice to this text? How do we honor the authority of the Bible here? As we saw, it is not by retaining the three-tiered world picture. For if we did, there would be very few people who would take the Bible seriously; even the strictest evangelical or fundamentalist, and the most conservative Roman Catholic, does not believe that the cosmos actually looks like the one shown in the picture above. And those who do believe it would not be taken seriously by the outside world. So, it will be clear that we do much more justice to this text by focusing on its *significance*: keep watch for idolatry because it can tempt you from all sides. Everything and everyone in heaven and on earth can irresponsibly instill a lot of fear in you. Or they could command so much respect that you are going to put your trust in them rather than in your God and Father. These could be very concrete objects (there are people who worship their horse as a god, or their canoe), but also more concrete things such as influence, pleasure, reputation, your job, or even your family. Therefore, watch out for things that are in vogue, and don't let them subdue you for there's only One that liberates you.

Seven Days

Now we have to take one other step. In verse 11 of Exodus 20 we encounter another thing related to the world picture as the people of Israel knew it at the time. In this we are not dealing with the structure of the cosmos, but with its *origin*. The words we want to examine will sound familiar to readers who are (or were) accustomed to hearing the Ten Commandments every Sunday: You must keep the day of the sabbath, "For in six days the LORD made heaven and earth, the sea, and all that in them is, and rested the seventh day: wherefore the LORD blessed the seventh day, and hallowed it" (KJV). For many Christians, this text alone is sufficient reason to reject any thinking that proposes a gradual development of life forms on earth. Heaven and earth and all that is in them, that is, all species were created by God in six days. While one can argue about the genre and literary features of Genesis 1, here, it seems, we are given a statement about which there cannot be any doubt. In addition, the Torah tells us that these words, like all the words of the Ten Commandments, were written by God himself on two stone tablets (Exod 32:15–16; see also Deut 4:13; 5:22). Why would anyone want to subtract any of it?

Nevertheless, a few comments need to be made about this topic. First of all, it is remarkable that in the book of Deuteronomy (which literally means "second law") the sabbath day commandment (Deut 5:12–14) is supported by a different motivation than in Exodus 20. Here it is not based on the creation in six days, but on God's liberation from slavery of his people in Egypt. Earlier in this chapter we already saw that the text of the Ten Commandments differs in other subtle ways from the account in Exodus. Therefore, the question arises, how are we to understand the differences between the two? Did God perhaps first give the version of Exodus 20 and, after Moses smashed the first tablets (Exod 32:19), give the Deuteronomy version on the second set God then wrote (Exod 34:1)? But would God have changed the second version of the Ten Commandments from the first? Was the first not good enough? That seems to be unlikely. Another scenario is more probable. Bible scholars assume that in both cases the justification for the sabbath commandment has been added to the original text by the author of the Bible book. Perhaps their explanatory words were intended as annotations placed in the margin of the text. It often happened that a person copying the text, consciously or unconsciously, included such a comment in the body of the text. We are not sure, of course, whether this also happened in this case. Alternatively, the motivations may have been added intentionally to the original text. In both scenarios, we may see the guidance of the Holy Spirit in such events.

In any case, the author or editor of the book of Exodus (unlike the author of Deuteronomy) made a connection between the Sabbath commandment and Genesis 2:1–3. That is, of course, an understandable connection because, according to Genesis 2, on the seventh day God himself rested from his work. So, the author actually says something like, "You must sanctify the Sabbath day, for according to your well-known creation story God, after six days of work, rested on the seventh day from his labor." Thus, for the author of Exodus, it is part of the message in Genesis 1 and 2 that God ordered not only space but also *time*. This is the purpose, then, of his words. Christians have taken this purpose seriously by taking the commandment for the Sabbath not only as a sign of God's covenant with Israel (see the motivation in Deut 5), but also as an institution that applies to all people. It is indeed clear that the interruption of the daily rhythm by a weekly day of rest is good and beneficial for everyone. We should be grateful that this institution was given to all people through Israel!

A Young Earth?

It should now be clear that the author of Exodus 20:11 did not quote the Genesis text with the intention of rejecting the idea of a gradual creation over millions of years. For that idea did not exist at all in his time. It was never his intention to reject something like the theory of evolution. That topic is not under discussion in the text and we should not "impose" it on it. It is probably true that the writer personally believed in a young earth, that is, in an earth that was created and furnished by God in a week. That is evident from the way he quotes the text in Genesis. But it is important to realize that it was not his intent to communicate that the creation occurred in six literal days; that is not the *significance* of the Genesis text. Rather, the authoritative message that he derives from Genesis 1–2 consists of the importance of the alternation of six working days and one rest day. The Exodus author's message is that according to the creation story, the organization of time is given to us by God himself and thus deserves to be followed.

The author's idea of a creation that was put into place over a short period of time, however, is not conveyed here as an authoritative message but as part of his world picture; we saw that this was also the case with his idea of waters under the earth. It is obvious, therefore, to assume that both "simply" belonged to the writer's world picture, a world picture that, we observed, shines through from time to time in various places of Scriptures. That is how the people of Israel saw things at that time, and so the author could simply refer to them in that way and be understood. World pictures do not only relate to the structure of the cosmos ("how is the world put together?") but also to its origins ("how and when did it come to be?").

Keeping these things in mind, we will discuss in chapter 4 how we are to read Genesis 1 in this regard. For also in interpreting this chapter, it is important that we pay close attention to the difference between *meaning* and *significance*. The actual and lasting *significance* of the text is crucial. If we would not make that distinction, then we are forced to retain the world picture illustrated above, and we would have to believe, for example, that there are bodies of water below and above the earth. But nobody believes that. Apparently, where it is obvious to us, we routinely make the distinction between meaning and significance (so this distinction is not a "trick" of contemporary theologians). But where it is not so obvious, the distinction may still have to be made. This need becomes clear when our current world picture starts to differ from that of the Bible author. Thus, it is somewhat arbitrary to make such a distinction between what the text literally says and what its intent is when interpreting Exodus 20:4 but not when interpreting Exodus 20:11.

But can we then go in any direction we wish with any Bible text? No. It is important to do justice to what the text wants to tell us. We cannot make it say whatever we want. The Bible itself does not allow an independent interpretation, as 2 Peter 1:20 clearly indicates. It therefore speaks of great respect for the text to not be satisfied with a superficial reading, but to continue to push for its actual meaning. When you do this, you are not forcing contemporary views upon the Bible but, instead, are listening as carefully as possible to what the Bible itself intends to say.

Discussion questions

1. "You shall not set your desires upon the Tesla of your neighbor." Mention the Ten Commandments one by one (perhaps divided in small groups of two or three) and try to substitute examples and concrete situations that might have occurred at the time these commandments were written with examples of our own time. Read the results aloud to

each other. What do these results mean to you? Do you feel estranged from the Ten Commandments, do they make more sense to you now, or does it make little difference?

2. Many people profess that you should read the Bible literally, from cover to cover. "It says what it says, and what it says is the way it is." Use Exodus 20:4 to show how you get stuck with this approach. How can you read this text using the idea that God adapted his revelation to the world picture of the time it was written?

3. Couldn't God simply have explained to the ancient Israelites how the world is put together instead of using language that was in keeping with their world picture? Why didn't he do that?

4. The American Old Testament scholar John Walton shows in several of his books how much the Israelites shared the world picture of their time. In a conversation I had with him, he told me, "The Bible is written for us, but not to us." Have a conversation about this statement. What do you think he meant? Do you agree with him? And what are the implications for our understanding of the Bible?

Group Activity

"The Bible authors were ordinary people, just like us." Is that statement correct? For yourself, give a number from 1 to 5 for this statement; a 1 if you agree with it entirely, a 2 if you agree with it somewhat, a 3 if you have no opinion on it, a 4 if you disagree somewhat, and a 5 if you completely disagree. Then tell each other which number you chose, and why. Discuss with each other the arguments that were given. At the end of the discussion do the exercise again, that is, give a number for the statement again. Is that number the same as before, or has the discussion changed your mind?

3

The Sun Stood Still

and Other Miracles

IN THE BIBLE WE encounter numerous miracles and miracle stories. A widely held view is that these stories do not agree well with contemporary science. One often hears that you have to choose: either you believe in the fairy-tale world of the Bible, along with its spirits and miracles, or you take science seriously. If you try to do justice to both the Bible and science, you will often be looked at with pity. You haven't quite understood the situation yet, for how can those two possibly be compatible! But if you persist, and ask why and how science actually excludes the possibility of miracles, the conversation often comes to a sudden stop. If you look for in-depth literature on this topic, you will soon notice that the discussion still revolves around objections to miracles that were first brought forward by important thinkers such as Baruch de Spinoza and David Hume. It seems, therefore, that the discussion is at an impasse (although many of Spinoza and Hume's objections have now been refuted), and that it depends much on the perspective that you start with; that is, do you or do you not take into account the possibility that God may act?

Read: Joshua 10:7–14

The Copernican Revolution

There has always been much controversy about Joshua 10, particularly about verse 13. The fact that Israel's enemies died in great numbers in their flight because at that very moment large hailstones fell from the sky (v. 11), was of course also a very unusual occurrence. One can certainly call it a great (and, in a way, a dreadful) miracle. But you hardly ever hear anyone talk about that. For all the attention is drawn to that other miracle: "the sun stood still" above Gibeon. Even the fact that the moon also stood still according to the story is much less known; after all, if the sun can stand still, it is no longer surprising that the moon can do this too. To be sure, the text itself already indicates the uniqueness of the sun miracle: "There has been no day like it before or since, when the Lord heeded a human voice . . ." (v. 14). Although the sun has stood still in other places in the Old Testament, and once even moved backwards for a short time (Isa 38:8), this was not at the request of a human being.

However, there is yet another reason why the miracle of the sun standing has still given rise to so much debate, and we will now discuss this in some more detail. For centuries, this text has been seen as confirmation of the so-called Aristotelian worldview as this had been elaborated in detail by the great Alexandrian astronomer and mathematician Claudius Ptolemy (second century AD). According to this worldview (or, better perhaps, *world picture*), the earth was the center of the universe.

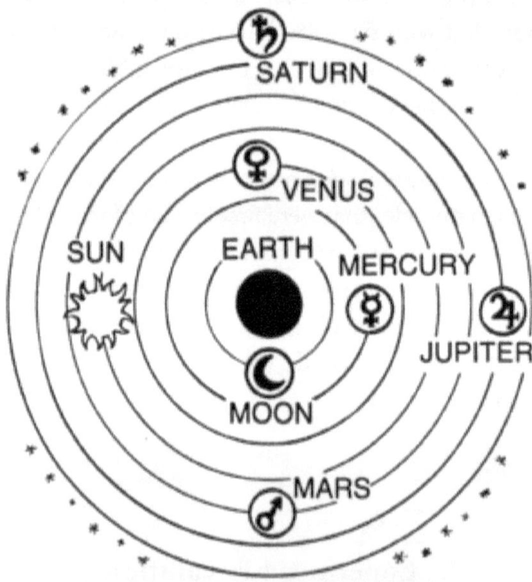

Fig. 2. A simple representation of the Aristotelian-Ptolemaic world picture. Not all planets in our solar system were known at that time.

As shown in Figure 2, the sun, stars, and planets moved in circular orbits around the earth, which in Ptolemy's view was a sphere, not a flat disc. Contrary to what is often thought, there have been very few Europeans through the centuries who believed that the earth was flat. Since the Greek philosopher Aristotle had provided evidence for a spherical earth, this continued to be the generally accepted view—also among church fathers such as Jerome, Ambrose, and Augustine. Very few people thought otherwise. Thus, it is incorrect to suggest that the spherical shape of the earth was only discovered when, in 1492, Columbus was the first to be brave enough to sail around the earth without being afraid of reaching the end of the earth and dropping off the edge. Columbus and his crew already knew that the earth was round, as did the scholars at the university in Salamanca, with whom Columbus discussed in advance the chances of success of his intended voyage of discovery.

What *is* correct is that the prevailing world picture was geocentric in nature until well into the seventeenth century. This means that the earth (*geo*) was considered to be the center of the universe. When the aforementioned Polish astronomer, Copernicus, determined that seeing the sun as the center of the solar system (which in his world picture coincided with the universe), this was certainly not accepted immediately by everyone. From a scientific point of view, Copernicus's view was not very strong initially. Ptolemy's system had raised all kinds of technical questions, but then, so did Copernicus's alternative.

It is very questionable whether Reformers such as Luther and Calvin opposed Copernicus's world picture, although they have often been blamed for this. But if they would have done so, this would have been perfectly reasonable. For in 1546 (the year of Luther's death) and 1564 (the year of Calvin's death) there was nothing to indicate that Copernicus might be correct. To date, only ten Copernicans have been identified between 1543—the year Copernicus's *On the Revolutions* appeared—and 1600! It was only after 1600, when Christian scientists such as Johannes Kepler and Galileo Galilei had adapted and experimentally tested Copernicus's theory, that this picture changed.

Voetius's Fear

Even then, however, it took a long time before the vast majority of Christians became convinced of *heliocentrism* (the idea that the sun is at the center of our solar system). That it took this long had, apart from the profound influence of Ptolemy, everything to do with our Bible text! After all, didn't Joshua 10:13 make it clear that the sun revolved around the earth? Well, then, the Copernicans were clearly in the wrong.

The well-known reformed theologian Gisbertus Voetius (1589–1676) took a very strong and combative stance on this point. For him, and for many of his contemporaries, it was an enormously important point. He reasoned as follows: if the Holy Spirit—the actual Author of the Bible—tells us something, then that must be correct. For the Holy Spirit doesn't lie. Well, the Holy Spirit tells us in Joshua 10 that the sun interrupted its movement around the earth. Then the sun must normally move around the earth, and thus the earth, not the sun, is at the center of the universe.

Voetius knew the view that we encountered in the previous Bible study, namely that the Holy Spirit would have adapted to the world picture of the first readers of the Bible. However, he did not find that thought acceptable. After all, those first readers, too, could easily have understood the difference between a sun that revolved around the earth and an earth that revolved around the sun. If the latter had been the case, the Bible could simply have recorded that. The patriarchs and the prophets were really not too stupid to understand the Copernican system! The Holy Spirit could simply have explained this to them, and through them all Bible readers would have been informed of the truth on this topic.

Voetius found the idea that the Holy Spirit would not have transmitted the truth to us in every detail of the Bible to be downright blasphemous. And when we put ourselves in Voetius's place, that is very understandable. For if one Bible text has to be interpreted differently from what it says, who says it's going to stop at that one text? And, indeed, it didn't. There are at least ten or so texts that assume a geostatic world picture—that is a world picture in which the world is immobile while the sun moves (see for example Eccl 1:5, Ps 19:7, 104:5, etc.). Voetius and his followers were therefore very concerned about the so-called domino effect, or "slippery slope." They were afraid that one thing would lead to another, and that, eventually, the meaning of no single Bible text would be certain.

Because the Bible is the book in which the salvation story and God's promises come to us, that is indeed an alarming thought! Nevertheless, Christians today don't have any problems with these texts. We have come to see that texts such as "The sun rises and the sun goes down" (Eccl 1:5) do not necessarily presuppose a certain world picture, but, instead, reflect the general human way of observing. Yes, the sun rises and sets; that's how we see it happening before our eyes—just as in our perception the earth does not move but is fixed. In this context, some talk of our "viewing image" or "perception image." There is no cosmological theory involved here at all. We say such things purely from our everyday experience. Even though we now know that the earth revolves around the sun instead of the other way around, we can still talk about a rising and setting sun, and we do so regularly. "What a beautiful sunset," we might say, for example. Well, in exactly the same way, Joshua could say, "Sun, stand still at Gibeon." When that subsequently happens (v. 13), that does not mean that the sun actually stopped orbiting around the earth, but that it stopped, *as seen from our observation point.*

The fear that Voetius and his students had, that once you deal with Bible texts in this way, there is no end to this process, has not come to pass. And no one believes any longer that you are weakening the authority of the Scriptures when you abandon the Ptolemaic world picture. To the contrary: we can now honestly admit that the so-called Copernican revolution (that is, the change in the world picture) has helped us to better understand how to read these kinds of texts in the Bible, because previously these texts were read "literally" instead of focusing on their intent. Apparently, the Holy Spirit does indeed lead the church "in all truth" (John 16:13) and can even use scientific discoveries for this. Let us not think too lightly about the creativity of God's Spirit!

Are Miracles Possible?

In the meantime, there is another problem with our text that many people today find hard to deal with. That is the widespread idea that miracles, from a scientific standpoint, can simply not occur. Isn't it outrageous to actually believe such things as are told in the biblical miracle stories? That sentiment is especially strong when it comes to miracles in which laws of nature seem to be broken. Even if we read the story of Joshua 10 in a non-geocentric way, it seems that some natural laws must have been broken (or temporarily suspended) if the visual effect of a nonmoving sun occurred indeed. As we will see, discussing this problem will move us beyond the topic of *world pictures* into considering the role of various *worldviews.*

Next to miracles in which laws of nature seem to be broken, there is another group of miracles that we can distinguish: so-called "coincidence miracles." We can still find these a bit more acceptable, because we all know that things can sometimes come together in a surprising way. A well-known example (introduced by R. F. Holland) is the story of the train engineer who at one point suffers a heart attack that causes him to lose his grip on the throttle so that the train automatically comes to a stop. When that happens right in front of a spot where a small child on a bicycle got stuck in the rails, so that the child's life is spared, we speak of a great miracle. It would be a great miracle indeed, of course (although it would also be complicated if the engineer would die of the heart attack—but that is another story); but it is not an impossible miracle in the sense that no laws of nature would have been broken. That is why we can still accept such a miracle that goes back to an accidental convergence of exceptional events.

It's a different case when we think about miracles that seem to *break* laws of nature. It is commonly thought that these kind of miracles—so-called "violation miracles" because they violate laws of nature—simply "cannot be." It is understandable, therefore, that Bible interpreters sometimes try to explain these miracles in terms of unusual circumstances (thus reducing them to "coincidence miracles"). For example, when we deal with the story of the Israelites passing through the Red Sea (or the Sea of Reeds) that is a possible option. It is conceivable that a rare natural phenomenon—in this case a strong wind that parted the waters—occurred at the time the Israelites had to pass through the water, and that the wind died down at the very time the Egyptians had also entered into the water. In fact, the Bible author mentions this (Exod 14:21). But in Joshua 10 we can't use this as an explanation. After all, it is not the case that once every so many thousand years the sun will come to a standstill, and then resume (in our perception) its movement again. That just doesn't happen. Here we really encounter a situation in which a law of nature temporarily doesn't govern in the usual way.

Is something like this extraordinarily unlikely? That is certainly the case. If that were not so, we wouldn't speak of a miracle. Water doesn't normally turn into wine, the dead do not arise as a daily occurrence, and the sun never stands still. You don't even need science to determine that. People always knew this. That's why we may be quite skeptical when we hear some kind of a contemporary miracle story (although this is sometimes difficult when the person tells the story with a great deal of conviction). There can be all kinds of reasons why something is not what it seems to be. Besides, people can sometimes be gullible, particularly when the miracle story is personal and beautiful. People can be deeply convinced of certain things that turn out to be wrong upon further reflection. Perhaps this has even happened to ourselves. For, after all, we're fallible human beings. But Christians do not need to be more naïve and gullible than others. As a Christian you want to accept things in good faith, but "good" in the sense of "on good grounds."

Good Grounds

Thus the question is: can you believe in miracles on good grounds? We have seen that this is certainly the case when we are considering "miracles of coincidence." Even when something is highly unlikely, it can nevertheless occur. This also applies to events that break a certain law of nature. We may even doubt whether it is correct to speak about "breaking" a law of nature. This suggests that a law of nature is an iron rule that can only be violated by some kind of supernatural force ("violation" indeed suggests the use of violence). But what is a law of nature really? Not more and not less than a pattern of repeated regularities. Series of events that regularly occur and that we can explain naturally (from cause-and-effect relationships). In a naturalistic worldview—in which only natural phenomena (matter, possibly spirit) exist—these laws of nature do indeed have the last word. There is, so to speak, no more to be said. Thus, if something happens that seems to go against a law of nature, then we have not fully explained the phenomena that the law governs and we have to reformulate either these phenomena or that law. In any case, the laws of nature determine what happens and what does not—and therefore also what can or cannot happen. The question of where the laws of nature come from usually goes unanswered. It is one of the difficult questions that atheism has to grapple with.

In a Christian (and more generally in a theistic) worldview, the question of the origin of the laws of nature does not go unanswered. In such a view they function as regularities that are instituted by God. Thus, we could designate them as "creational laws" and consider them to be part of God's upholding care as alluded to in, for example Colossians 1:17 ("all things holding together" in Christ). Already in Genesis, God guarantees the dependable changing of the seasons (Gen 8:22). The laws that govern these seasonal changes also fall under God's providential care. But if God instituted the laws of nature, and still upholds them, then of course he is not bound by them and can also act in ways that are not governed by these laws. The Reformed American philosopher Alvin Plantinga has famously said that in a miracle, God does things differently from the way he usually does them.

There are good reasons why miracles do not occur very often. For that would make reality unreliable. For example, if we were always to be rescued from dangerous predicaments, we would not develop a sense of responsibility. And if nature would act one way at one time, and in another way at another time, we wouldn't be able to depend on it. Let's be grateful for the laws of nature for they make normal life possible! But miracles *are* possible. That is to say: if you already believe in God, then it is not strange to believe that the world is open to God's actions. Many normally functioning people (including people with higher education) indicate that they have actually experienced miracles. While they can be mistaken, it is not reasonable to assume in advance that this is the case by definition. In his well-known book on miracles (*Miracles*, 1947), C. S. Lewis shows that the question of whether we believe in miracles is indeed strongly related to our worldview.

When our worldview is "open" in the sense that we take into account the possibility of God acting, this acting can take place both within the bounds of nature as they are known to us, or beyond those bounds. In doing so, we cannot dismiss the possibility that there are underlying laws of nature that we do not know, but which God can use. In any case, that would not be strange. We humans, too, can use certain laws of nature in such a way that they influence the functioning of other laws. For example, when a ball falls out of a tree, that movement is usually stopped by the ground on which it lands, in accordance with the law of gravity. However, when I stick out my hand and catch the ball, that doesn't happen. The ball does not fall on the ground but stays in my hand. Have I broken or violated the law of gravity? No, gravity only had a different outcome because the upward pressure of my hand countered its effect. Believers assume that God can act in similar ways. Thus, laws of nature are not so much "broken" (violently or not), but God may use them in exceptional ways. The only difference is that in the case of God's acting, we cannot trace the way in which God achieves his purpose because we cannot perceive his ways with the world. It is his secret. We cannot explain it. We can only marvel at it.

In the same way we could take the miracles that are narrated in Joshua 10. We cannot explain them, since if the earth would indeed have stopped moving around the sun for a while, normally our planet would not have survived. Yet, in ways we cannot fathom, God may have prevented its being torn apart. We just know too little to be able to exclude such scenarios.

No "God of the Gaps"

That sense of wonder is also appropriate when God acts in an "ordinary way," in accordance with the laws of nature that we know. For that is possible too. We now know a lot about how a new human life begins and how it comes into the world. We understand all kinds of natural factors that play a role in this process and can even control some of them. Nevertheless, in a Christian community we thank God when a child is born to one of its members. And rightly so. With Psalm 139, we praise him "who knit me together in my mother's womb." For even though this phrase is intended to be a metaphor and we know how babies come into this world, we can still see God's hand in it. We can be grateful that God can also use the "ordinary" (but in fact very special) course of events. In classical theological language we can say: As a "first cause," God can use all kinds of "second causes" that function on a different level. The things that occur according to the laws of nature can also awaken a sense of wonder in us. A field of flowers can speak to us in a way that a conversation cannot. That is all the more true for the gigantic universe and the microscopic quantum world.

Psalm 29 tells us that God speaks through a thunderstorm. We may find that primitive nowadays. After all, we know the causes of thunderstorms, don't we? Nevertheless, we do not have to play faith and science off against each other. For even though we understand the causes of thunderstorms today, God can still speak to us through them. A scholar who worked in a university, a person of faith, once applied for a higher position. He would have had a significant salary increase, become a full professor, and his students would have looked up to him even more. But he hesitated. Would he be happy in his new position? Would there be people with whom he could speak from heart to heart, and would he be able to work on things that really mattered to him? As a Christian, he had prayed about these things. As he drove home after the interview, which had gone well, a violent thunderstorm suddenly broke out over his head. That made the difference. He knew: I should not accept this job. And he did not. Later he became a professor elsewhere, in an environment where his work matched his talents more fully. So, for the person who can hear and understand, God can speak still speak through a thunderstorm.

For another reason, too, it is important that we don't limit God's actions to miracles. If we only see God at work in extraordinary events, we run the risk of seeing his work less and less as we can explain more events naturally. The space left for God will become progressively smaller as science advances. Atheist thinkers like to present it this way: "We used to think that God had created all animal species, but now we know that they have all originated by evolution." As if these two are mutually exclusive! Why would God not be able to use gradual processes in his work of creation? Anyone who sees God only in miracles will soon be left with a "God of the gaps": we see God at work where science has no explanations. That can lead us to try to keep those gaps open at all costs. Then we turn against science as soon as it comes with a good natural explanation. But as a believer you will always lose that fight eventually. For this reason, it is much better to see that God can be at work—to our good—through all kinds of natural processes.

Miracles as Signs

When we now look once more at the miracles in the Bible, we see that the relationship with the laws of nature is hardly mentioned. Apparently, that has become much more *our* problem. Rather, it is striking that miracles tell us something about *God's* character and intentions. They are never just strong acts but always signs. Thus, miracles have a referring character. They show us that we can depend on God—or, in the case of miracles of judgement (such as the deadly hailstones in Joshua 10), that we have to take God into account. In both the Old and the New Testament, miracles are in the service of God's liberating actions. Even the miracles of judgment show us that the devil, death, and evil do not have the last word, but that God lives and reigns. That is why miracles are always encouraging and strengthen our faith.

In the New Testament the miracles of Jesus show us his unique status and mission, and demonstrate the beginning of the kingdom that he proclaimed: God's new world, where there will be no more sickness, sorrow, and death. Miracles show that God is able to make that new world begin. In that sense they are never capricious or random. They always occur in the framework of salvation history. They point towards God's future. Similarly, we may also look at particular miracle stories that occur today—stories that can withstand scrutiny and that are in agreement with what we know about God's nature and intentions. On this point, various miracles in which Christians believe are also different than the many miracle stories and legends that make the rounds in various religious traditions (including the Christian) and that are often no more than strange stories.

This brings us back to Joshua 10. For when we think about it, the miracle of the sun that stood still is also a sign of God's acts of salvation. Although, of course, we have our questions about the violence that accompanied it (but, as said, that is a different topic), here too the miracle serves God's liberating deeds. God helps Joshua to set the city of Gibeon free from the five armies that have besieged it. And if it requires a miracle to establish Joshua's name and fame, then that miracle is given to him. In this connection, it is significant for Christians that Joshua is the Hebrew version of the name Jesus. For Jesus, too, came to liberate the people who—like Gibeon, by their own fault, incidentally—had been captured by the forces of evil. And when a unique miracle was needed to establish the name of Jesus permanently among the nations, that was given to Jesus: God raised him from the dead.

Discussion Questions

1. Have you ever experienced a miracle yourself? If not, do you regret that? If yes, what makes you convinced that it really was a miracle given by God? Was it a "miracle of coincidence" or was it completely unexplainable scientifically?

2. Do you understand the fear of Voetius described above? In this connection, try to articulate what the Bible means to you. What place does the Bible have in your faith life?

3. God can still speak to us through things that happen, such as a sudden thunderstorm, we suggested above. In this connection, what do you think of the example of the job interview? Do you know other examples? How do you prevent explaining all kinds of events in such a way that they serve your own views, and in so doing, that you make God subservient to your purposes?

4. The stories about the resurrection of Jesus and other miracles in the Bible differ from each other (say from one Gospel to another) in details. At times it is impossible to make the various versions agree with each other. To what extent is that problematic for believing these miracles?

5. Suppose someone tells you about a miracle that happened to him or her. What determines whether or not you believe that person? In

other words, what criteria would you use to determine whether a divine miracle could have happened?

Group Activity

Divide yourselves within the space in which your group finds itself. Stand on the one side of the space if you are of the opinion that miracles no longer occur today. They did occur in Bible times, but today God speaks through his Word and no longer through miracles. If you think that there is a special intervention by God once in a while, then you stand a little more towards the middle. And if you think that many miracles happen, but that we often don't see them, go and stand on the other side of the room. Then explain to each other why you stood in the place that you did. When everyone has had a chance to speak, ask if there are people who, having heard what everyone has said, want to stand in a different spot upon further reflection.

4

The Creation of the Cosmos

ON CHRISTMAS EVE OF 1968, astronauts orbit the moon for the first time in history. From Apollo 8 they present a live report of the sunrise on the moon and take the first ever color photos of planet earth. What they see makes a huge impression on them and on all those who are watching them on earth. Then the crew does something they had already included in the flight plan: they begin to recite the first few verses of Genesis 1. Eighty-six hours and seven minutes after the launch there were the familiar words: "In the beginning God created the heavens and the earth." Commander Frank Borman, pilot Jim Lovell, and moon landing specialist William Anders took turns in the Scripture reading, breathlessly listened to by millions on earth. While science had said farewell long ago to the worldview of Genesis 1, at this moment of human technological achievement, the text seemed to uniquely meet the deeply felt human need for meaning.

Read: Genesis 1:1—2:3

Six Days and a Sabbath

The text of Genesis 1 has been the topic of much discussion throughout the centuries. Since it became the opening chapter of the Hebrew and Christian Bible it has always drawn extra attention (like the opening sentences of a sermon, which are often listened to with the most interest). Interpretations of the chapter are as numerous and varied as the discussions about it.

The church fathers already saw it as a virtue to write extensive discussions about each of the creation days (so-called *hexamera,* or "six-day books"). Also today, Genesis 1 still finds itself in all kinds of animated discussions. Young earth creationists in the Christian, Jewish, and Islamic world regard a so-called literal reading of the text as a litmus test for orthodoxy. Conversely, militant atheists like to pin down the monotheistic religions on precisely such a literal reading. In this way, they seek to dismiss any faith in God as ridiculous, because it is completely disproven by scientifically established facts.

Those who seek an intermediate position between these two extremes run the risk of not being heard, because any nuanced opinion will quickly be dismissed by the general public as too complicated. As a result of all this, it is difficult to read this chapter with an open mind. Those who are going to read it often have a preconceived idea about which way they want to go, or not go, with it—and will certainly have an idea what the chapter is about. However, all this can stand in the way of letting the text speak to us. Bible scholars often rue the fact that the text can hardly get a foot in the door because it has been hijacked by the discussion about creation and/or evolution. And they have a point. Inadvertently, we tend to read the text through glasses that focus on the question: what is factually correct and what isn't (where the percentages can vary between 0 and 100 percent)? And all the things that the text can tell us outside of that topic can easily escape our notice. Even if it is impossible to read Genesis 1 without prejudice, it is still rewarding to hear what is being said, and how that would have sounded in the ears of the first readers.

It's easy to lose sight of the beauty of the passage, as the following story shows. A chaplain at a Canadian university spoke to a biology professor. The professor asked the chaplain if he was familiar with Genesis, because he was often asked by young earth creationist students about Genesis 1. He mentioned to the chaplain that he had never read Genesis, and, as an atheist, was reluctant to do so. But he also thought he should be familiar with it. The chaplain gave him a Bible and told him that they could read it together if he wanted. The biology professor read Genesis 1—for the first time in his life—and when he looked up there were tears streaming down his face. "That's the most beautiful thing I have ever read," he said.

When we do read it with an open mind, it quickly becomes clear that Genesis 1 is no ordinary, prosaic text. From a literary point of view, the chapter (which, strictly speaking, extends to Genesis 2:4a) has a clear and fascinating structure. After the opening verses (more on those later), the account of each of the creation days contains some sentences that are structured in the same way:

- The passage for every day begins with "And God said."

- Then God *makes* what he just said he was going to make and "it was so"; it is through God's creative word that all things come into being.

- In the case of the first three days, God also gives names to what he has made.

- Six times, viz. after a creating act, it is stated, "And God saw that it was good"; the seventh time, this happens in a superlative step: "God saw everything that he had made, and indeed, it was very good." Thus, the seventh time is the climax, just as the seventh creation day: the day of the Sabbath.

- The day texts are all closed with the same formula: "And there was evening and there was morning, the x-th day."

- In regards to style or genre, we are dealing here with artistic prose. Genesis 1 is not a poem or song, but it certainly does not have the style of a historical account of events either. It has been stylized, and the acts and events described have been placed in a particular *framework*. Of course, that has not been done without a reason. The writer or writers wanted to convey a message to the reader.

The Framework Interpretation

What the text of Genesis 1 wants to communicate becomes clear when we pay attention to the framework that is used to structure the various creation acts of God. There appears to be a remarkable connection between days one, two, and three, on the one hand, and days four, five, and six, on the other. In the first three days a certain space is created each time, which is then filled in the second series of three days. In schematic form, this pattern looks like this:

	The space created	The space filled	
Day 1	Light separated from darkness	Sun and moon placed in it	Day 4
Day 2	Rainwater separated from seawater	Aquatic animals and birds placed in it	Day 5
Day 3	Land separated from water	Animals and people placed on it	Day 6
Day 7 The Sabbath as climax			

If you read the text literally, such an overview raises quite a number of questions. For example, how could there already be light on earth (day 1) when the sun and moon had yet to be created (day 4)? And how are we to think about part of the water on earth being pulled upward by God, as it were, and being placed above the fixed dome in the sky, the "firmament" (day 2)? But in the perspective of the Eastern world picture that we encountered in the previous chapters, this is all perfectly understandable. It is the language of the first readers that is being used here. It is important, therefore, that when we read this chapter, we keep in mind who it was written for. After all, the Old Testament is, initially, the book of and for the people of Israel in the ancient Near East. Today, by God's grace, we are allowed to read the mail, as it were, along with those to whom it was first addressed. God's creation work is described in language that uses *their* world picture, so that *they* could understand it. And what they heard, above all, was that the God who revealed himself to Abraham, Isaac, and Jacob, is the one who created heaven and earth with all that is in it. To him be all honor!

The Unique Voice of Genesis 1

Genesis 1 is a powerful chorale that opens the Bible with a unique cosmogony (a story of how the world came into being). When we compare it to the cosmogonies of lands and cultures surrounding Israel, we get a better understanding of its meaning. The cosmogonies of these lands are similar in some ways to the one of Genesis 1, but in some crucial ways they differ remarkably.

First of all, in these other stories there are unreliable gods who are usually occupied with trying to outdo both each other and human beings. As a human, you therefore had to fear the whims of the gods. They were usually quite selfish—just like people. In the God we meet in Genesis 1, however, this is by no means the case. To the contrary, the Creator devotes much affection and care to his creatures. He is by no means selfish but loves them, apparently. This is especially the case for humans, who are a distinct object of God's love. The human species is given a special environment in which they can live and thrive and develop themselves. At the same time, they are creatures surrounded by many others. Humans were not even created on a separate day, but together with the land animals. Thus, Genesis 1 keeps us humble. It's not human beings who are the crown of creation, as is often said, but the Sabbath: the entire week ends at the mighty moment when God can rest from his work. The situation is then completely safe and ordered, so that God can make an entrance, so to speak, and begin to reside in this home that he has built so beautifully. The world is like a cosmic temple, in which God is on the throne and human beings may serve as priests (the inauguration of a new temple often took seven days in the ancient Near East).

Second, in various ancient Eastern cultures, as we already saw in a previous chapter, the celestial bodies were often revered as deities. These Easterners were especially impressed by the power and heat of the sun, as well as by the phases of the moon. They were therefore inclined to think that you had to keep on the good side of those imposing celestial bodies, and keep them satisfied with sacrifices and other forms of worship. Taking a totally different position, the author of Genesis 1 deprives the celestial bodies of their mythical properties. Shamash and Yareach (Sun and Moon) are not even given a name. Here they are simply called the two great lights, next to the smaller stars (v. 16). All these heavenly bodies have been placed by God, like numerous pinheads, onto the dome (the "firmament") he created. That's where they will circle in their orbits from now on. Clearly, the heavenly bodies are ordinary creatures and certainly not gods. Thus, the author of Genesis 1 reacts polemically against the paganism of the countries that surround Israel. In fact, he "Christianizes," as it were, the origin stories that circulated in these countries—taking over their world picture but filling this with a religious alternative that recognizes the God of Israel. Jews and Christians believe to this day that the writer was inspired by God's Spirit. The way in which God makes himself known to us here in Genesis

1 is special and impressive indeed. It may even serve as model for how we should engage today with widely shared ideas and theories that circulate in our own culture. Perhaps we should not reject these out of hand, but qualify their secular character by grounding their substance in God's creative activity.

The unique nature of Genesis 1 is also evident from a third and final difference between this text and similar texts from Israel's surrounding nations. In other ancient Eastern origin stories, the deity is invariably involved in a bloody *fight* with other cosmic primal forces. These were often represented as dragons or similar monsters that had the sea as their natural habitat. These forces offered enormous resistance to the deity, so that the creation work was accompanied with much violence. It is striking that this resistance is still somewhat noticeable in Genesis 1, but that God does not need any violence to overcome it.

The chapter begins by speaking about the chaos and emptiness of the earth. According to the Hebrew words used here (pronounced as tohu wavohu; one hears the dark sounds), these present a certain threat, as did the flood (*tehoom*), which is mentioned directly afterwards (v. 2). In other Old Testament texts, which we wrongly often undervalue, you can see traces of these threatening forces more clearly (e.g., Job 26:12; 38:8–11; Ps 74:13–14; Isa 51:9). But also in Genesis 1, it is noticeable that God is not finished immediately with the chaotic powers. To the contrary, step by step, he creates order on earth. First, light and darkness are separated, then water and water, and, finally, water and land. God's creation work consists, first of all, of separating what does not belong together, of good and evil. Only then will there be forming and filling. In this way, the chaotic initial state will gradually turn into a livable whole that is "very good."

Powerful Care

You may even wonder whether Genesis 1 actually refers to a "creation out of nothing" (*ex nihilo*), or whether this doctrine is more firmly based on other biblical texts (e.g., Ps 33:6, 9; Heb 11:3). Many Bible scholars suggest that we should consider Genesis 1:1 to be an inscription above the entire chapter. That is, in the vein of "When God created the heavens and the earth, it happened like this" (not unlike the words chosen in the NRSV). The actual narrative would then begin in verse 2, where the earth, which already exists, is covered with water, and is in a disordered state. In this state God intervenes with his creation work. Indeed, Genesis 1 is mainly about the ordering and functioning of the earth's matter, even though we cannot substitute that totally for the bringing into being of new things (the verb *bara*, to create, actually refers to "bringing something into being," and is only used for God). The Douay-Rheims Bible (a Roman Catholic Bible translation from the sixteenth to seventeenth centuries) expresses Genesis 2:1 as: "So the heavens and the earth were finished, and all the furniture of them." The reference to furniture is apt here. The flora (v. 12) as well as the fauna (v. 24) are brought forth from the already existing earth, but the celestial bodies (v. 16) as well as the human beings (v. 24) are two examples of creatures that are apparently made by God *ex nihilo*. In any case, it is important to see that God's creative work encompasses more than just the *making* of things. That is why we speak about "the creation of the cosmos" (like the creation of a work of art, which requires much creativity because one has to work with preexisting materials) rather than its "making."

In the meantime, subsequent Bible authors, particularly in the New Testament, rightly concluded that God must be the one who is responsible for the existence of *all* matter. "By faith we understand that the universe was formed at God's command, so that what is seen was not made out of what was visible," the author of Hebrews states (11:3). Similarly, according to John 1:3, *all things* were made through "the Word of God," while Colossians 1:16 identifies that Word with Christ: "for in him all things in heaven and on earth were created, things visible and invisible." Also in Genesis 1, God's creating and formative power is of course enormous. Hence, no more violence or bloody battles are needed when God dismantles the threatening primordial flood and brings the barren earth to fruitfulness. To the contrary, here too it seems to be true: "Not by might, nor by power, but by my spirit," it will be done (Zech 4:6). It is God's Spirit or *ruach* who awakens life of the dead cosmos (Gen 1:2; see also Ps 104:30) and brings things to their destiny. Yet, the reminiscences of a primordial chaos in Genesis 1 still remind us of the mysteriousness of evil: we are not being told where evil originated—just that it somehow was there, that God has taken it seriously and is able to overcome it, step by step creating cosmos out of chaos.

The careful way in which God acts in Genesis 1 also has something to say to us about how we deal with the earth. In verse 26, human beings are appointed to be image bearers of God, and to rule over creation. In this way, we are called to be God's representatives on earth. In the way we rule creation, we are to reflect the way God interacts with creation. These well-known words are therefore not a free pass to exploit the earth for our own comfort, but, in fact, to demonstrate the same strong care that has first been shown to us by the Creator. Without using destructive force, God ordered the wilderness that was the earth, and gave every creature a proper place. The outcome was that a great and varied wealth of living creatures became possible—that is, an incredible biodiversity. Genesis 1 suddenly brings us a very relevant message, for if we take contemporary climate science seriously, we become aware of the disastrous effects of pollution and increased emission of greenhouse gases caused by human activities. Among the negative results of these human-caused changes in our environment is a great decrease in biodiversity. This goes directly against the task that God has given us in Genesis 1.

The only way to get this message is to read and listen carefully. It is striking that in this context people are presented with a variety of vegetarian foods as their diet (v. 29). Meat is not included. That is allowed only later (as a temporary emergency measure?), directly after the great flood (Gen 9:1–3). It apparently does not fit in with the "very good" of God's creation.

Genesis 1 and the Big Bang

It will be clear that when we read Genesis 1 this way, it does not compete with contemporary scientific views about the origin of our cosmos. For its meaning remains intact, even though we believe that in the creation of "heaven and earth" the processes took a different course than what the ancient Eastern Israelite imagined. World pictures come and go, but the Word of God endures forever. In the meantime, it is good to realize how vastly our contemporary world picture differs from the one of Genesis 1. That will prevent us from attempting, consciously or not, to make the two overlap in some way. Such attempts have often been made and still have a following, but they are not convincing because they are contrived. This applies, for example, to the interpretation that sees the days of Genesis 1 as periods of millions of years. That is creative, but it is not a satisfactory solution. Neither is the assumption of the existence of a long period of time between verse 1 and verse 2, in which the dinosaurs, etc., would have lived and been destroyed. For that, the world pictures are just too divergent, and it is more truthful to simply admit that. Nevertheless, even without such "attempts at harmonization," there are striking parallels between the message of Genesis

1 and contemporary science. To discover that, we will now examine more closely the contemporary scientific theory about the origin of the cosmos.

As cosmologists and physicists now see it, the universe emerged from an exceedingly hot and dense point some 13.8 billion years ago. This age has been calculated using three different methods that are not related to each other. Because experts arrived at broadly the same time frame, science is fairly certain in this regard (and the calculations are becoming more and more accurate). The theory is based on the fact that *expansion* of the universe was observed. It turned out that the galaxies and celestial bodies in our cosmos are moving farther and farther apart. Compare it to the baking of a cake; as the cake mix starts to rise, the currants and raisins (read: the celestial bodies, as far as they are not joined together through gravitational force) become increasingly more distant from each other. This process continues to occur in the universe.

The Belgian priest and physicist George Lemaître, in 1931, calculated back in time, and concluded that the universe must have begun at a point zero—perhaps with the explosion of a primal atom. He reasoned that the universe, including space and time, must have originated by way of this "Big Bang." The phrase Big Bang was not introduced by Lemaître (and for good reasons: strictly speaking the event was neither big nor a bang), but later, in 1949, by the British cosmologist Fred Hoyle. As we shall see, Hoyle would have nothing to do with this novel theory and intended "Big Bang" to be a denigrating term.

Now the idea that the universe had a beginning was revolutionary indeed. The prevailing idea at the time was that space and time, energy and matter had always existed. The universe was thought to be eternal, with neither a beginning nor an end. Many scholars—not only Hoyle, but also Albert Einstein, no less—therefore could not join Lemaître and his supporters and rejected the new theory. They held on to the idea of a static universe (that is, a universe that does not expand or implode) and tried to "save the appearances." They suggested that somehow new matter was constantly added, so that the universe would be, despite its expansion, in a kind of permanent equilibrium (a steady state or stable condition).

However, this view would gradually lose ground to the Big Bang theory. For it followed from Lemaître's calculation that certain effects of the Big Bang would still be observable in the universe today. Therefore, he could add a prediction to his theory. Lo and behold, in 1965 this "cosmic background radiation" was indeed found. Predictions based on the steady state theory, to the contrary, turned out to be incorrect. For this reason, the vast majority of experts gradually became convinced of the correctness of the Big Bang theory. Of course, many questions remain; for example, about what exactly happened during the first fraction of the very first second; and also about how the whole process will end. For if the universe has a beginning, it is likely that it will also have an end. There is indeed much speculation about how and when that will occur (see more on this in chapter 7).

Harmony between Cosmology and the Belief in Creation

George Lemaître himself was wary to make a connection between his Christian faith and his scientific ideas. For him, the two were more or less separate topics. Others, however, have been surprised from the beginning at the noticeable parallel between the Big Bang theory and the message of Genesis 1. For central to that message is that the world has not always existed (as influential Greek philosophers, and, in their footsteps multiple Western thinkers, believed), but that, at some point, it had begun to exist. That is exactly what the Big Bang theory also says.

According to the Christian faith, God made the cosmos, it is his creation. To be sure, today's cosmology does not point unequivocally to God as the creator of the universe. Even though there is much that points to an extraordinarily mighty, personal spiritual being that has brought the cosmos into being, God's creation work does not allow itself to be scientifically verified. Having arrived at this point, science has to remain silent. But science does absolutely leave room here for the belief that God stands at this beginning, and in a way, it even explicitly evokes that realization. Some atheistic cosmologists were acutely aware of this. The aforementioned Fred Hoyle, for example, admitted generously that the Big Bang theory reminded him too much of a belief in creation and a Creator God. He himself remained a faithful believer in the alternative, the steady state theory. But as we saw, that theory turned out to be unconvincing.

There's another point that is relevant here. Recent cosmology also demonstrates how infinitesimally small the probability is that conscious life could have originated somewhere in the universe. Numerous physical factors must have exactly the right values to make that life possible. In this context we can talk about the *fine tuning* of the universe. From a scientific point of view, it is a great miracle that a planet that sustains life, and even intelligent life such as human beings, came into existence at all. There are many moments in the history of the universe when things could have gone in a different direction. In fact, there were quite a few instances when that was very close.

In the novel *Dawn* (2022—which, just like this book, was translated by Harry Cook), Corien Oranje, Cees Dekker, and I try to capture the unbelievably thrilling features of these cosmic events in story form. In doing so, we are able to show the similarities with the way the Bible tells the creation story. For in Genesis 1 too, it becomes clear how much care the Creator has taken to ensure that, in the midst of all the other life forms, human beings would be there. From the beginning, God has set up the creation so that this would be the case. And also in the Bible, a history follows in which the continuation of life and of God's covenant with humanity often hangs on by a thread. In the relationship between God, humanity, and creation, things could have ended much differently, and it is a miracle that we're still here. This is all due to the fact that God shows his faithfulness by holding on to human beings no matter what happens, and by making sure his plans with the cosmos come to fulfillment. Indeed, he is the Lord "who made heaven and earth, who keeps faith forever, and does not forsake the work of his hands."

Considering all this, it is not surprising that in 1968, at the appropriate moment, the text of Genesis 1 was sent to earth from Apollo 8. The unmeasurable empty space of the universe, with its unimaginable distances and deep secrets, confuses and baffles us. We live on a beautiful but tiny and vulnerable planet somewhere in an insignificant hinterland of the cosmos. In some ways, we don't amount to much, just like the fledgling people of Israel (Deut 26:5) or the emerging Christian community (1 Cor 1:26). And yet . . . the message of Genesis 1 gives things meaning, and it shows our lives to be immensely valuable. We are wanted and meant to be here. By faith we discover that this universe was brought into being through the Word of God. With Genesis 1 we say therefore: to him be all glory and honor.

Questions for Discussion

1. By interpreting Genesis 1 in terms of the "framework theory," there is no tension between this chapter and contemporary science. This relatively recent interpretation was proposed by the Dutch Old Testament scholar Arie Noordzij, in 1924. How likely is it that this theory is

correct? Discuss the possibility that this theory is proposed by scholars who do not want to choose between Bible and science, but also discuss the possibility that the natural sciences may have helped us to better understand the meaning of Genesis 1.

2. In this chapter it is suggested that not all biblical authors believed the same things about how God created the universe. Some, such as the author of Genesis 1, may have believed in the existence of "primordial matter," whereas others (like authors of the New Testament letters) claimed that in the beginning God created all there is. Do you think it is possible, and (given the enormous differences in time and place between them) perhaps even probable, that the biblical writers held slightly different views in this respect? Or would you rather argue that Holy Spirit made them speak with one voice?

3. Many believers regret that the interpretation of Genesis 1 given above requires quite a bit of knowledge about the context in which this text was written. They have the feeling that the Bible has been taken away from them because they can no longer read "just what it says." To what extent is this concern valid? In this regard, also discuss the task of theologians and preachers.

4. What do *you* think it means that human beings are image bearers of God? And how is that connected to the current environmental and climate crisis?

5. Do you think the Big Bang theory is a confirmation of the creation belief expressed in Genesis 1? Or do you see more of a threat in this theory?

Group Activity

We have seen that there are other texts in the Bible that speak about God's creation work next to Genesis 1–2. These texts tend to be undervalued compared to Genesis, even though theologically (that is, in what they teach us about God) they are not necessarily less important. Divide the following texts among small groups of two to four persons. Take the time to let your text sink in. Then discuss in your small group what you learn about God's creating work that is different or complementary to Genesis 1. Also pay attention to the nature of your text. For example, is it a text that describes or praises the work of God? Is it intended to be read literally or are images used that help us to speak in awe and praise about God's power of creation? Afterward, share your findings with the whole group.

1. Job 38:4–11
2. Psalm 74:12–17
3. Psalm 104:1–9, 19–24
4. Isaiah 40:25–31
5. Colossians 1:15–20
6. 1 Timothy 4:1–5

5

The Molding of Man

IN GENESIS 2 WE encounter the man named Adam. In this same chapter, Adam receives his wife from God's hand; she is called Eve from chapter 3 on. These two persons are known as the first couple of human beings to exist: Adam and Eve, our first two ancestors. But *did* they ever exist? Contemporary science tells a different story about the origin of humans, and that story seems irreconcilable with the one of Genesis 2. There is no trace of Adam and Eve in the scientific narrative. Although there are discussions of the so-called "mitochondrial Eve"—the woman from whom we have all descended along the maternal line, at this moment dated some 155,000 years ago—scientists have been quick to point out that she cannot be equated with biblical Eve. Should we therefore just abandon Adam and Eve, and see them as a bit of religious folklore—one of the circulating colorful old myths about how our species began? Or is there another way of looking at it? Let's see where the Bible text will take us.

Read: Genesis 2:4–25

Two Creation Accounts

When after reading Genesis 1 you continue into Genesis 2, you notice a change in atmosphere and writing style a few verses into that second chapter. The first three verses clearly belong to the narrative of chapter 1. These describe what happened on the seventh day of the creation week and conclude the preceding account. After that, we no longer hear anything about the various creation days. Instead, the main body of Genesis 2 zooms in on the creation of the first man (vv. 4b–7; 1:26–29 dealt with humanity as a whole, as a species or "kind," as it were), the planting of a garden (2:8–17), and the search for a partner for the man (vv. 18–25). All of this is preceded by a small but intriguing sentence at the beginning of verse 4: "These are the generations (*toledoth*) of the heavens and the earth when they were created." It is important to note that "generations" here does not refer to what went before but to what came after; literally, in this phrase the term means: that what was produced by the heavens and the earth. Similar *toledoth*-sentences occur in several places in the book of Genesis. They always appear to have an initiating function, and thus delineate a certain text unit. The next time such a phrase occurs is in 5:1. Thus, apparently, we are to read Genesis 2:4 through to the end of chapter 4 as one unit. And, indeed, chapter 2 cannot be separated from chapter 3, and neither of them from chapter 4.

In the case of 2:4a, there is also a clear reference to 1:1, since the phrase "the heavens and the earth" and the verb "created" from 1:1 are repeated. Commentators therefore rightly think that the verse is inserted by a later editor or redactor (sometimes identified with the writer of Genesis 1) to connect the preceding creation story (1:1—2:3) with the following one (2:4b—4:26). Interestingly, according to 2:4b this second story is about the "making" (that is, forming, molding) of "the earth and the heavens." This time, the earth is placed up front instead of the heavens, and indeed the earth will take center stage in Genesis 2–3. Yet, the focus in these chapters is not on planet earth as a whole, but on a very specific place on it: the garden of Eden. Like all gardens, this garden is supposed to be a bounded place. Apparently, it wasn't the whole world that was a paradise. Rather, God prepared a deeply harmonious place for the man and woman as a "beachhead" in a world that still had to be subdued (Gen 1:28), whereas the garden of Eden itself only had to be tilled and kept (Gen 2:15).

Indeed, when it comes to the relationship between Genesis 1 and 2, it is often thought that Genesis 2 continues the theme of 1:27, by functioning as a hyperlink to it, so to speak. Thus, if you click on "So God created humankind in his image," then you read in chapter 2 how that happened. Genesis 2 would then provide further details on the sixth day. This thought has to be approached with some caution, however, and we will therefore not develop it here. Careful reading of the texts is sufficient to see the differences. For example, according to Genesis 2, human beings were created before the flora (v. 4–5) and fauna (v. 19). According to Genesis 1, however, it was the other way around: on the third day the plant kingdom was created, on the fifth and sixth day the animal kingdom, and it was only at the end of the sixth day that human beings made their appearance. Thus, these two accounts do not agree with each other. In the past, there have been artificial attempts to make them agree by translating some verbal forms in Genesis 2 a bit differently, so that it seemed that also in this chapter the man was created last. But all commonly used English translations of Genesis 2 rightly opt for a more natural reading of the text, according to which Adam already existed before land animals and birds were created. For example, the NRSV renders v. 19 as follows: "So out of the ground the LORD God formed every animal of the field and every bird of the air, and brought them to the man to see what he would call them; and whatever the man called every living creature, that was its name." It is quite clear here that Adam already existed at the moment the animals were created—which shows that the order of creation in Genesis 2 differs from that in Genesis 1.

It is noticeable, furthermore, that chapter 1 always refers to "God," whereas from chapter 2:4 on, the covenant name, "LORD," precedes "God." In Hebrew, the texts give the name that should not be spoken and which, for that reason, is not provided with vowels: YHWH. In order to prevent that this name is spoken nevertheless (for example by saying the four consonants in succession), Bible translators follow the Jewish example of writing "Lord." That name appears for the first time in Genesis 2, while there is in this and the next chapter no longer mention "God" by itself, as in Genesis 1. In short, all indications are that Genesis 2–4 has, historically, a somewhat different background than Genesis 1, and that we are therefore dealing with two creation accounts that were merged at some point and have been adjusted to each other here and there. That would not be exceptional, because that is also the case with other Old testament passages. In this case, it seems probable that the editor(s) added the word "God" (Hebrew: *Elohim*) to "YHWH" in Genesis 2–3, in order to indicate that YHWH as spoken of in Genesis 2–3 is the same one as the God spoken of in Genesis 1 (in Genesis 4, he stops doing so, since by then this should be clear to the reader). This suggests that Genesis 2–4 is older than Genesis 1; perhaps the writer of Genesis 1 preambled the existing story about Adam and Eve with his own story, thus deliberately situating Genesis 2–3 in the much wider context of God's creation of the entire universe.

However this may be, it is clear that we should read neither Genesis 1 nor Genesis 2 with the aim of trying to answer this historical question, "What happened first, and what did God do then?" (for then we will get stuck), but more with this theological question in mind: "What are we being told here about the relationships between God, humankind, and the world?" Then the chapters complement each other and both enrich us, instead of contradicting each other. From a historical point of view, it is good to know that the strictly literal approach to the first chapters of the Bible is only of recent date. Certainly, Christians in earlier centuries generally assumed that the text was a representation of historical events; but the emphasis did not lie there for them. The actual meaning and intention of the text was sought and found on a deeper, spiritual level. As they saw it, the text recounts what we were meant to be by God, what became of us as the result of sin, and how God is yet not leaving us in our predicament (Gen 3:15).

It was not until the early twentieth century, when modern theology had broadened its influence and all kinds of changes had taken place in society, that certain groups of Christians began to dig in their heels. At that point, great emphasis came to be placed on a literal interpretation of the first chapters of Genesis, as if these reported a series of events in an exact historical way. In this context, scientific significance began to be given to Noah's flood (Gen 7–8) as an explanation for the numerous fossils that had been found by then. The "creationist movement," which promoted these views, began in the United States. Creationist Christians there came to be called "fundamentalists" and their ideas spread to many places around the world. Since then, it has become difficult to read the first chapters of Genesis with an open mind, as had been possible in the past. Augustine, for example, on the one hand believed—over against the Aristotelian-Ptolemaic world picture (see above, chapter 2)—that there were waters above the firmament, since Scripture told him so (Gen 1:6–7). On the other hand, he considered that the notion of a creation in six days must be meant symbolically, because the almighty God would not need six days to create the world—in reality God probably created heaven and earth in the blink of an eye!

Pre-Adamites?

How exactly did those who put the book of Genesis together want to relate the two creation accounts to each other? They did not want to make them into one grand story (because in that case they could easily have reconciled the differences in the sequence of the various creation works). But the *toledoth* formula in Genesis 2:4 that we mentioned earlier does suggest that they wanted to have the second creation account placed in the time *after* the first. For that is almost always the case when two passages in Genesis are separated by this formula. A story that occurs after the *toledoth* formula never overlaps, in time, with a story that occurs before the *toledoth*. To be sure, a later story can at times refer back to an earlier one in order to continue the thread. Thus, it is not necessarily the case that the creation of Adam and Eve in chapter 2 took place only after that of humankind as a whole in chapter 1. Adam and Eve can also be seen as *included* in the people "created male and female" in chapter 1. Chapter 2 then discusses how that happened in their case, and what their specific role would be. So this can be the element of truth in the traditional view that Genesis 2–3 elaborates on Genesis 1:27.

In concrete terms this means, however, that Genesis 1:26–28 deals with the creation of far more people than only Adam and Eve. After all, the Genesis 1 text seems to be about the creation of human beings in general (i.e., of humankind, though the author deliberately avoids the word "kind" in this connection). Some interpreters go even further by seeing the two creation accounts as consecutive in time. Then the people referred to in Genesis 1 would be "pre-Adamites," that is, human beings who were created in God's image before Adam and Eve. That idea (first suggested in the seventeenth century by the French Huguenot Calvinist Isaac La Peyrère) is quite appealing from a scientific point of view. But based on the texts it is rather speculative. What is not speculative is the idea that Genesis 1 includes more people than just Adam and Eve, who are the focus of Genesis 2 and 3. Likewise, the Genesis 2 and 3 narrative zooms in on a limited part of the cosmos that was ordered in Genesis 1, namely the garden of Eden, Adam and Eve's home.

Later in the opening chapters of Genesis we indeed find quite a few indications of the existence of contemporaries of Adam and Eve who do not seem to be their descendants. For example, Cain has a wife (4:17). Now you can suspect that this was his sister, and that this, at the time, did not constitute incest (seeing it as a temporary provision to get the human species going). But then you have to make numerous assumptions about matters that the text does not inform us about. We also read that, after his murder of Abel, Cain is afraid that "anyone who meets me may kill me"

(4:14). Who would that be, exactly? The expression ". . . anyone who . . ." makes it clear that Cain is not thinking just of his parents (his brother Seth was not born yet at that time). To top it all off, Cain then proceeds to build a city (4:17). The language used here can only refer to a settlement with quite a few inhabitants. In short, the text of Genesis 2–4 does not suggest that all people at the time of Adam and Eve and their offspring are descended from Adam and Eve, although the text has often been read that way (e.g., based on Genesis 5:1–2, where in another *toledoth* formula the editor once more weaves together the stories of Genesis 1 and 2).

As said, Genesis 2 also makes it clear that the place where Adam and Eve live is a rather specific one, namely the garden of Eden, somewhere "in the East" (v. 8). By giving this specification, the chapter is again open to the possibility that other people may have lived outside the garden. Yet, Adam is "the man" (v. 7) who, together with his wife, Eve, who joins him at his side, is the couple of interest in chapter 2. With these two people God enters into a special relationship—call it a covenant. As the story continues, Eve is called "the mother of all living" (Gen 3:20). This does not necessarily refer to all people (just as it does not literally mean "of all living beings"), but she is in a sense the mother of all those, who, coming after Adam and Eve, were also called to live in a personal relationship with God. It is striking in this regard that Adam is not only a personal name but also means "the human being." Adam represents *this* human being, as it has been created in God's image: the fully developed human being with whom God can and will make a covenant.

The fact that Adam is called "the first man" in other places in the Bible also refers to this representative function: he represents with God all people of his kind. In a similar way, Christ is called the "last Adam/human being" (1 Cor 15:45), even though many other people lived around him. The fact that Christ is the "last human" does not even negate that many other humans would still come. Similarly, the fact that Adam is called the "first man" does not exclude that many other human-like people may have lived before him and around him. Making this kind of observation is not to engage in a strained attempt to "harmonize" Scripture and contemporary science—it is to try to do justice to what the biblical texts do and do not imply. The view that there are two particular creation accounts in Genesis 1 and 2 goes back, as we said, to the middle of the seventeenth century. At that time, the theory of evolution lay far in the future, and the most remarkable fossils had yet to be found. There was no influence of science upon the reading of these texts, unless it came from newly emerging views in biblical scholarship. Yet it is significant that an interpretation of Genesis that has room for the possibility that Adam and Eve were not our only and oldest ancestors is in line with what we now know from science about human origins.

For a good understanding of the text, it is also important to note that Genesis 2–3 uses quite a bit of ancient Eastern symbolism about the creation of humankind. The chapters provide an outline of an important phase in the ancient history of humankind in pictures that are typical for the time in which it was written. From a cultural-historical point of view, this was not the very earliest period in which the human species existed. For arguably the agricultural practices that figure in Genesis 2–4 (see, e.g., 4:2) were preceded by hunter-gatherer cultures in which humans did not yet cultivate farmlands. So, in pictures that are typical for a later phase in human history (the agrarian phase), we are told about some events that happened at the beginning of human history. One can compare this to way in which for example the sixteenth-century Dutch artist Pieter Bruegel the Older painted the arrival of Joseph and Mary in Bethlehem in the framework of the Dutch winter landscape (including snow) with which he was familiar. In other words, it is the genre of Genesis 2–4 that suggests that we should not read these chapters in a literal-historical way.

The genre of Genesis 1–11 as a whole has aptly been referred to as "mytho-historical" (e.g., by the well-known Christian apologist William Lane Craig). The historical intention of these chapters is especially clear from the genealogies that they contain in Genesis 5, 10, and 11—passages that link Adam and Eve directly to Abraham and thus to the people of Israel. It is difficult to separate the figurative or mythical elements neatly from the ones that are to be taken literally, but, for example, the two trees that are located in the garden of Eden clearly have a mythical background. Such trees figure in other ancient Near Eastern stories of origin in various ways, and what stands out about them is that they have a magical working. In Genesis 2–3, it seems that the tree of the knowledge of good and evil automatically offers such knowledge to any person who eats from its fruits; neither can the tree of life be stopped from offering eternal life to Adam and Eve in case they would eat from it after they had fallen into sin (Gen 3:22). Clearly, such magical trees do not exist in real life.

This is not to suggest that such figurative elements are meaningless for us—to the contrary! But their meaning should be found in what they convey: the first tree represents the human possibility to become morally guilty, and the second tree conveys the possibility to gain eternal life upon remaining morally upright. Thus, the tree of knowledge of good and evil suggests that the story is about the stage of human evolution in which humans became morally responsible persons. The primates that preceded humankind no doubt did terrible things, but they could not be held accountable for these, since they did not have a discrete knowledge of good and evil. Such knowledge only arose with the emergence of humans like us. As to the tree of life, we will expand a bit on its meaning and relevance in chapter 7.

The Scientific Story

When we look at the contemporary scientific story about the origin of *Homo sapiens*, it looks much more complex than the account of Genesis 2. That's not surprising. We even encounter that more often when we dig a bit deeper into Bible stories. We know, for example, that there were many more socio-economic aspects to the story of Kings Omri and Ahab than are told in the Bible (1 Kgs 16:21–34). The authors of the Bible simply emphasized some aspects of the events. Because they wanted to accentuate these aspects, they left out other matters. In this way, the author(s) of Genesis also wanted to highlight particular aspects, and we will, of course, come back to these accents as they figure in Genesis 2–3.

We will first look, however, at the broad picture of contemporary theories of human origins. Paleoanthropologists (scientists who study human evolution on the basis of fossils and archaeological finds), biologists, and other natural scientists generally agree that human beings have evolved from earlier species through processes that took place over millions of years. Although we do not "descend from the apes," we do have ancestors in common with them. About six to seven million years ago, the branch that led to the evolution of human beings split off from the branch that led to the chimpanzee, the animal that, of all species, has the most features in common with us. The first representatives of *Homo sapiens* are said to have originated from ancestral hominins—as they are called—some 200,000 years ago. That original group of humans in Africa is thought to have been quite small: an estimated 10,000 to 12,500 reproductively active individuals, not counting those who did not have offspring and thus did not leave genetic contributions to the population. In later times, small groups of people left the parent population in Africa, and spread out across Asia and Europe and, later, also across North and South America.

Of One Blood

Although we are uncertain about all kinds of data and dates (and sometimes have to revise our opinions about them), the main outlines of the scientific theories of evolution of human beings are nevertheless generally agreed upon. They are based first of all on the fossil record that has accumulated over the last few centuries, that is, on the remains of countless organisms that have been preserved in the earth. The relationship between the various hominin fossil species is not always clear, but the line towards skeletons that resemble our own is unmistakable. Then, second, in more recent times there has been the evidence that comes from the comparison of genetic material (DNA) between and within the various species (for example between Neanderthals and recent human beings). The low level of genetic variation within the human species indicates that we have all descended from the same African population.

One could say that all of this confirms what Luke reports about a speech by Paul, who stated that God "hath made of one blood all nations of men . . ." (KJV), or, as the NRSV puts it, "[f]rom one ancestor he made all nations . . ." (Acts 17:26). This, once again, is an interesting form of "consonance" between faith and science. But it will also be clear that the contemporary scientific account about the origins of the human race differs considerably from the interpretation of Genesis 2 to 4 that has been held through the ages. From a scientific point of view, for example, it is impossible that the entire human race originated from just one single pair of ancestors. Species never arise from just two individuals. Rather, they "pop up" in groups in a certain niche where the conditions are favorable. Moreover, the first humans, as they emerged some 200,000 years ago, were certainly not as communicative and culturally developed as Adam and Eve and their children according to Genesis 2 to 4.

Seen from an evolutionary perspective, you therefore have to say that Adam and Eve reflect a later phase in the history of human development, a time when *Homo sapiens* was developing a culture with music and metal tools (see Gen 4:21–22). According to some experts, this culture developed relatively rapidly, so that one can speak of a "cultural Big Bang." This must supposedly have taken place about 45,000 years ago (the art on the walls of the famous caves of Lascaux bears witness to this). Others deny or qualify the sudden, dramatic nature of these events and assume a much more gradual development of human culture. Still others identify Adam and Eve with *Homo heidelbergensis,* which preceded *Homo sapiens* as well as the Neanderthals, living some 750,000 years ago. However this may be, it is impossible to determine when Adam and Eve lived—for that, the image that Genesis 2 to 4 conjures up is too imprecise. In fact, these chapters comprise of what is sometimes called "reverse prophecy." Inspired by the Spirit, the Bible author makes striking pronouncements—not about what will take place in the future (as is usually the case with prophecy) but about what took place at some time long ago. This cannot, and does not have to be, dated on the historical timeline.

What is possible from a scientific point of view, though, is that all people presently on earth have Adam and Eve as an ancestor. To be sure, in that case we are not descendants of Adam and Eve alone, but also of numerous contemporaries of theirs. All of us have many ancestors (two parents, four grandparents, eight great-grandparents, etc.), so as we go back further in time, we also share more and more ancestors; after all, my great-grandparents are also the ancestors of all kinds of other people. Recent calculations have shown that if we go back in time in this way about five thousand years, we arrive at a common ancestor who is shared by all people that are alive today. Of course, we have a great many other ancestors, and the genes of this one common ancestor have become so "diluted" throughout the generations that it is difficult to find a trace of them. Yet, in that sense Adam and Eve may well be the ancestors (albeit not the only ones) of all the people that lived in New Testament times, and thus also of us. That turns out not to be impossible, as has sometimes been thought.

Most significant is that both in the Bible and in contemporary science, humankind is seen as a unity. It is incorrect that the various races of humanity each have their own origin, an idea that has long been a source of racism. According to the Bible as well as contemporary science, we are all "out of one blood" (Acts 17:26) or "cut from the same cloth."

God's Special Care for Humanity

It is interesting to list these similarities and differences of science and Scriptures, and to compare them side by side. More important, however, is to learn to read the Genesis 2 text on its own merits, quite apart from the science and, as we did for Genesis 1, to probe for what the Holy Spirit wants to tell us in it. What becomes clear then, for example, is the special care that is given to the creation of Adam and his wife. It is exceptional to see the Creator get down on his knees in order to fashion this special creature. For we read that God formed the first human being "from the dust of the ground." The image that is given to us here is of a potter who sits with his knees in the mud and works the moist soil (v. 6), kneading it carefully into the shape of a human being. The animals are formed later in the same way (v. 19). They too have been given the breath of life and are therefore "living creatures" (see also 1:20). But this spirit (*nephesh*) is blown by God only into the human being—a very striking image that can give much food for thought. One wonders: is it perhaps this special act of God and the relationship that is established by it that makes humankind unique in respect to other species? In any case, through this act what was only the inert human form is now brought to life.

It is clear that the Creator is spoken of here in very human terms. Possibly the image of God as a potter was known in Israel at the time from its ancient Eastern neighbors, particularly Egypt; the image is used later in the Old Testament, for example in Isaiah 64:8 and Jeremiah 18:1–6. Be that as it may, it will not have been taken literally in Israel but symbolically. After all, the God of Israel cannot be depicted in any form, and does not have physical hands. Even today, there is hardly anyone who reads Genesis 2:7 literally. What is the intent of this text, and what are we being told here? According to many, the first humans were created *separately* by God and did not emerge from the animal world, as the theory of evolution suggests. However, it is questionable whether that is part of the message here.

In any case, these words and pictures indicate that human beings were not put on earth "out of the blue," but that there were processes that led to their being there. They came to be out of existing matter. That this must be directly from the earth and cannot be from animals (which are themselves formed from the earth) is not the critical point here. The deep connection of human beings with the earth is essential, however. That is also clear from the wordplay that is used here: "earth" in Hebrew is *adamâ*, which has the same root as Adam; Adam's job is to till the ground (v. 15). Human, animal, and earth are inextricably related. Hence, human beings, just like the animals, will return to the earth: for "you are dust, and to dust you shall return" (3:19). This deep mutual connectedness between humans, animals, and the earth that Genesis shows us is, of course, highly relevant today. We cannot squander the earth's beauty and well-being, cause animal and plant species to become endangered or extinct, and reduce biodiversity in ecosystems without repercussions. That is not only a sin against the Creator, but it also greatly endangers our own future. The deep connectedness of humanity's fate with the earth can thus already be discerned in the Genesis text, reflecting a wisdom that by far precedes us.

Meanwhile, how we humans came into existence continues to be an indescribable miracle—both in science and in the Bible. That we are to be grateful to God for this miracle is what Genesis 2 expresses in a touching way. Not only has God created our bodies, but God has also seen to it that we have a mind that is intrinsically connected to our body, so that the human person became a balanced unity of body and mind. When we think of the origin of human beings along an evolutionary pathway, then here too, it is important that we do justice to the specific role of the human spirit or soul. The human spirit makes us more than matter, more than an ennobled animal, and connects us in a special way to God. Our highly evolved human consciousness makes it possible for God to address us as the only one among all his creatures with whom God can build a mutual relationship of love, trust, and devotion.

Today, too, we are therefore encouraged by this passage; we did not appear on earth by chance, by a disinterested fate. The "random mutations" that are part of Darwin's evolution theory are not independent from God's providential care. And what is true for Adam and Eve is also valid for us (see Ps 103:14): we are vulnerable people, but wanted by God and intended to live on God's good earth. For he has sculpted us with much love and care so that we would live for him. The garden of Eden was intended to be a holy place in which Adam and Eve could serve God as priests. Just like the priests that were to come later, they were allowed to live on what the temple (in this case the garden) yielded as food; and they were called upon to return praise to God and be a blessing to the earth.

Adam's Vision

Finally, God's care for Adam and for all humans is also evident in Genesis 2 in another way. Although the man may have been "wonderfully made" (Ps 139:14), it turns out that he is spiritually lonely. While according to Genesis 1:31 everything was very good, there seems to be one thing that is "not good" (vs. 18; here, too, we have an indication that Genesis 1 and

2 are two separate creation accounts). The animals do not appear to be a suitable partner for the human being. The man needs someone who is his equal and a match for him, and someone to whom he feels attracted. To meet this need, God goes to work once more, now as a *builder*. He takes the rib—or, as some old translations would have it, the side—of Adam, and makes it into a woman (2:21). Adam is delighted with the result, and the two immediately form a tight twosome. How are we to imagine this? Is Eve actually made from one of Adam's ribs? Or is she made from one half (side) of him, and that Adam then got a new side in its place? Once again, the text itself suggests that we should not take it so literally. For the text states that Adam fell into a "deep sleep." In Hebrew a word is used here (*tardema*) that indicates a trance-like state (the Greek translation has: ecstasy). The only other time the word is used in Genesis is in 15:12, where Abram has a wondrous night vision. That seems to be the case here too.

Adam learns in an exceptional way, that is through the vision, how much Eve is his equal. Not his drudge or subordinate, as men often treated women, but of equal worth as himself, a worthy match. Yes, his helper, but in the way that God himself is called the helper of humans (for example, in Ps 146:5). God has brought Eve to him, Adam is shown in his vision. And it is God's intent that they will always stay together. Later, Jesus will say that God has instituted marriage here as an unbreakable union (Matt 19:4–6). It's clear that this part of Genesis 2 does not lose any of its powerful message when we know it to be a vision. In fact, as we also saw for Genesis 1, its actual meaning even dawns upon us with more strength and clarity. For we are no longer distracted by speculations about what we are to think about what was going on with Adam's rib but can more directly focus on the message: God intended married men and women to be in a lifelong relationship with each other, and all people—married or not—to live in supportive and close relationships. The way that Jesus deals with this passage in Matthew 19 does not require a more literal interpretation either but points us to this main thrust of the text.

Questions for Discussion

1. That we, human beings, have descended from organisms in the animal kingdom (hominins) has not been scientifically "proven" but is a very probable result of all kinds of research. Many pieces of the puzzle fall

into place when we assume that to be the case. Some Christians have a strong aversion to this idea, however. Why do you think that is? To what extent is this aversion understandable?

2. We see in Genesis 2 how closely the human species is connected to the earth, and also to the animal world; the fates of humans, animals, and earth are closely interconnected. What does this tell us in a time of ecological crises?

3. Do you agree that the two special trees in the garden of Eden, the tree of life, and the tree of knowledge of good and evil, should not be seen as literal trees? What do you think is their meaning in Genesis 2–3?

4. It is not always easy to determine where in Genesis 2 the language is symbolic and where the first readers took passages in a more literal way. Why do you think it is helpful in situations like this to especially look for the *intent* of what we are reading, that is, the message that is conveyed?

Group Activity

It is difficult at times to read the Bible afresh. That is certainly the case with well-known passages, such as Genesis 2. Ever since kindergarten we think we know, more or less, what it says and don't expect much that is new. To break through this "laziness" it can be helpful to read the text again in a concentrated way and to use the so-called Swedish method in doing so. This method consists of three parts: 1. Underline words or expressions that stand out for you (where you thought: Hey, I never really knew that this is what it said). 2. Put an exclamation mark in places that you find particularly important or beautiful. 3. Put a question mark by what you don't understand. When you have taken some time to do this, discuss with each other the places where you have underlined, placed exclamation marks, and placed question marks.

6

The Evolution of Sin and Death

IN THE PREVIOUS TWO Bible studies we saw how beautifully the Creator furnished the world and with how much love and care he created humankind. Nevertheless, when we look around us, the world is not always beautiful and human beings are not always charming. To the contrary: the world abounds in death and destruction. Through the ages, people have done an enormous amount of harm, and it doesn't seem to be getting any better (it's just the opposite, you would sometimes think). Where does this spiral of negativity on earth come from? Some say it has always been there. Sin and evil, death and destruction are simply part of life. From an evolutionary viewpoint, how could it be otherwise?, they say. Others question or deny that. All the things that detract from the good life cannot have been part of God's good creation, they think. They were added later, as foreign intruders. How are we to see that? How have sin and death "evolved" (i.e., developed) on earth?

Read: Romans 5:12–21

What Paul Does in Romans 5

Before we discuss the complicated passage in Romans that we will examine, it is important to first see the context in which it occurs, because (as is often the case) this larger context will help us understand its meaning. In Romans 1 to 3 Paul concluded that the moral qualities of humankind are not good, and that this applies to both gentiles (Rom 1) and Jews (Rom 2). With all people, everywhere, it had gone wrong ever since Adam and Eve. From there it went from bad to worse (Gen 5–11). That is why God called Abram (Gen 12), and made an agreement with him—a covenant—in order to make a new start through him and his descendants. That too became a dismal failure. Thus, no hope remained: all people have sinned and will have to do without God's glorious presence (Rom 3:23). That is dramatic, because it tells us it's not going to end well for us. At the same time, the Old Testament is full of God's promises that show God does not intend to let his creation and creatures come to a bad end.

In Romans 3:21 this severe tension in Paul's comments had come to a solution: God continued his faithfulness to his covenant promises (or, as it is called here, his justice) in the life and death of Jesus Christ. And he has done that for Jews *and* gentiles. Romans 4 and the first part of Romans 5 dealt with the personal trust in Jesus as the way in which these two groups can be taken up into God's covenant of grace. Through the connection we have with Jesus through faith, the hope of the glorious nearness of God returns (5:2). For it is Jesus who reconciles us to God, already now (5:11). How much more will he rescue us then, later (5:10)! Then, in Romans 5:12–21, Paul takes one last look at this whole series of events—before continuing to work out what the Christian life consists of (chapters 6–8). Not unlike what you might do after you experience something very tense, something that narrowly turned out well. Then when it's all over, you realize that you crawled through the eye of a needle. You put everything that happened—how you ended up with big problems, but also how you were rescued unexpectedly—on a list. That is what Paul does in this passage.

In Romans, Paul's main aim is to highlight the salvation that Christ has brought to us. For he is deeply impressed by that. What God has done in Christ is so fantastic! We have that one person to thank for our salvation. Paul discusses, in a powerful chiaroscuro (light-and-dark) picture, the time when evil came into the world—how sin and death, by way of Adam, entered into the world long ago. It is not Paul's intent to present a doctrine here about sin and death as topics in themselves. No, everything he writes about these topics is marked by "the triumph of grace" that has been accomplished, thanks to the work of Jesus. It is important to establish that while this passage leads all too often to discussions about Adam, original sin, etc., it is often overlooked that these topics are not the point of Paul's discussion. For the main point here is Christ, and the grace of God that can be found in him. This is not to say that the rest is irrelevant, but that we should not cut it loose from what mattered most to Paul!

It Is All about Christ

That being said, it is now time to consider what Paul is exactly saying in our passage. That is not so easy, because the passage starts with a so-called *anacoluthon*—that's a sentence that starts well but doesn't end well grammatically. In this case, Paul stops his thought at the end of verse 12. Suddenly the train stops for a moment. Most translations do indicate this; some, like the NRSV, even put a hyphen there. It *is* clear what Paul was going to say, for that becomes clear in verse 18, where Paul picks up the thread again. He wants to say that just as the sin and transgression of one person brings death (v. 12) and condemnation (v. 18) into the world, so the rescue from death and condemnation was also accomplished by one person. With that first person, Paul is referring to Adam (a little later in the text, his name is mentioned), while the second is referring to Jesus. However, before he finishes the thought started in verse 12, Paul is suddenly reminded of some possible misunderstanding that he wants to avoid. Otherwise, the reader might get a totally wrong idea. He therefore interrupts the train of his thought, discussing the first misunderstanding in verses 13 and 14, and the second in verses 15 to 17.

The first thing that Paul wants to prevent is that the readers would think after verse 12: if death is the result of the transgression of a divine law, then what about those who have not transgressed such a law? Moses received the law for all the people of Israel at Sinai (Exod 20). But the people who lived before him—except for Adam who received a law in Genesis 2:7—did not have one. And there were quite a few: all of Genesis and half of Exodus discusses many of them. They did sin in the sense that they did things that were morally wrong, but they did not violate commandments (or "law") as Adam did. Therefore, their sins were not imputed to them, says Paul. For these generations, Paul relativizes the relationship between sin and death. That these people died, he says, was not because of their sin. He does not say why they did die, but reading verse 12, it is likely that Paul saw their deaths as a result of *Adam's* sin.

The second misunderstanding that Paul wants to prevent is the idea that all Christ did while he was on earth was to restore what Adam and his progeny had broken. In fact, what Christ did (vv. 15, 17) is much greater than setting Adam's wrongdoings aright. After all, the grace that he brought to our world doesn't only cover Adam's transgression and its effects, but also all later transgressions. It is thus infinitely more valuable and abundant. It also helps us to progress, instead of taking us back in time. For the gift of Christ's grace helps human beings to become the caretakers of creation that they were intended to be from the outset. Later, in life eternal, humans will finally "exercise dominion in life" (v. 17). That is to say, humankind will rule over creation like a good king, so that creation can come to be what it is meant to be (for this relationship between humankind and creation, also see 8:21). In short, God's covenant will finally be able to fully unfold and come into its own.

After this long aside, Paul returns to his main theme (vv. 18–21). This brings out that, in spite of all differences, there is also a parallel between Christ and Adam: Christ brought life into the world through his gift of grace. Adam, through his sinful deeds, brought death. The question we now face is whether the latter—that Adam brought death into the world—is contrary to what we know from science today, or, at least, what we think we know.

No Life without Death

In one of the previous chapters, we discussed the Big Bang. An interesting comparison gives a good indication of the immense periods of time that have passed between the time the Big Bang occurred and the appearance of humans on earth. If you set the time between the Big Bang, some 13.8 billion years ago, and today as one year, then you can put the Big Bang down for the beginning of January 1. At that moment the universe was "born." The Milky Way, which is visible from earth as a milk-colored band, and which consists of billions of stars including our solar system, was formed on April 1. Our sun with its planets, including the earth, did not follow until September 9. On December 19, the first fish and vertebrates were formed on earth, and the multicellular plants on December 20. One or two days later, insects and reptiles made their appearance. The dinosaurs arrive on December 24, only to become extinct on December 28 as a result of a meteorite impact. By December 26, mammals came on the scene, and a day later, the birds. It's not until December 31 at 10:30 PM that human beings follow. So we are real latecomers. In relation to the other creatures, we have only been here a very short time; plants and animals preceded us. In this example (as in Genesis 1) we've been here only a few days, but in reality, many millions of years.

You may wonder, of course, how certain all of this is. I obtained these numbers from a book now published quite a few years ago (T. X. Thuan, *The Birth of the Universe: The Big Bang and After*, 1993). The precise dating will probably have changed in details, over time. But the big picture has remained intact, and is still being confirmed. No matter how you look at it, the conclusion that the earth is very old, and the universe a number of times older, is difficult to escape. Even young earth creationists sometimes admit that if we examine the empirical data honestly, everything points to an old earth on which there have been living organisms for many millions of years (the reasons that they nevertheless do not believe that are completely related to their interpretation of the Bible).

Now suppose that life has indeed been present on earth for millions of years. Then that must also be true for death. For where there is life, death is never far away. If there would have been life but no death, the earth would have been covered in no time with a layer of autotrophic bacteria (these bacteria, which grow at an exponential rate, feed themselves without using other organic matter). No other form of life would have been able to develop. Therefore, from the moment there were living organisms on earth, these organisms must also have died at some point. And this cycle of life and death has continued, also when the most beautiful birds and mammals and later the hominins, appeared on earth.

The Death of Plants and Animals

Now we heard Paul say that death only came into the world through the sin of Adam. Hasn't that been hopelessly refuted? Does that perhaps belong to the worldview of his time, a view that is no longer ours? Let us not jump to conclusions. In Romans 5, Paul discusses the death of human beings. Unlike in Romans 8, he is not discussing plants and animals here. When he speaks of death, he limits himself to human death. For he writes in verse 12 that, since Adam, death has come to all *people*. The death of animals is not being discussed here. The plants and animals that had already died, quite apart from human sin, therefore do not disprove what Paul writes here, and they are completely unconnected to the topic of this chapter. It is also not contrary to what Paul writes elsewhere (Rom 6:23; 1 Cor 15:21–22) and what is said in other parts of the Bible.

Many Christians believe that after the human fall into sin a sort of "cosmic fall" took place, as a result of which some animals turned into predators, and death and destruction entered into the world. In itself, there is an idea worth considering there: our human sin has enormous negative impacts for our natural environment, including the animals. For example, they suffer from our boundless drive for growth. However, a cosmic fall in the sense of a sudden or gradual origin of carnivorous animals after the fall into sin is not mentioned in the Bible. Not even, for example, in Genesis 3:17–18, where God curses the earth "because of you" (Adam), and where God tells Adam that the earth will produce "thorns and thistles." This does not mean that the earth suddenly started to function differently, but that Adam had to go from paradise to the hard-to-work ground, and he would certainly notice the difference. And even if that meant that this was the first time that thorns and thistles would grow, that is not quite the same thing as animals dying for the first time.

In one of the other creation texts, Psalm 104, verse 21 mentions that predation is a part of creation for which God is praised. We may wonder whether the suffering and killing of beautiful animals fits in with the "very good" of Genesis 1:31. But the question is, of course, what that expression means. According to Numbers 14:7, the promised land was "a very good land" (as it literally states). That did not alter the fact that at that time the land was full of enemies, and idolators, not to mention thorns and thistles, and predatory animals. The expression here clearly means that the land was *potentially* very good. It could be cultivated so that it would have lush vegetation and feed all the people. That seems to be precisely the thought in Genesis 1. What God created can function as God intended. The earth is a home in which humans will be able to flourish. That doesn't preclude that plants and animals have always died in their time, thus making place for other organisms.

The Death of Human Beings

From a biological point of view, humans are no exception to the unbreakable rule, "without death, no life." This would imply that people, too, have died since the time they lived on earth. This also applies to our hominin ancestors and our "cousins." As to the latter group, we can think of Neanderthals—a subspecies of *Homo sapiens* that we find traces of, according to some, in Genesis 6:1–4. Neanderthals lived alongside modern human beings a long time ago, and there is evidence that there was some genetic exchange (based on sexual intercourse) between the two *Homo* lineages. Paul states, however, that the death of us humans is the result of our sin, and not the result of the biological nature we share with nonhuman organisms. In this context, Paul assigns a crucial role to Adam, the first person to sin. Through Adam's fall it's all corrupted! It is sometimes said that in this way Paul read more into Genesis 2 and 3 than what it says. But, in any case, what he writes agrees with Genesis 2:17, where God says, "of the tree of the knowledge of good and evil you shall not eat, for in the day that you eat of it you shall die." Here, too, human death is seen as punishment for Adam's transgression of the command.

It has always amazed interpreters that the threat of Genesis 2:17 has, strictly speaking, not come to pass. For according to the Bible story, Adam and Eve did not die on the day that they fell into sin, but only many years later. For this reason it is often thought that "dying" here does not refer to physical death, but to what you might call *spiritual* death—and that would then be what Paul is also referring to in Romans 5. We do, indeed, see that from the moment Adam and Eve sinned, the relationship with their Creator is broken. The relationship with each other is also negatively affected in all kinds of ways. The community in which we as people flourish appears to be disturbed, and our dealings with the earth have become difficult and problematic (Gen 3:17–19). We even have great difficulties with viruses. In short, from the moment of the fall, we have become estranged from our source of life, with all the results that this brings. We are spiritually dead.

"Death" in the Bible is what we call a layered concept. It has multiple dimensions of meaning and you always have to carefully determine the context to see which aspects are and are not relevant in a particular discussion. Elsewhere in the Bible, for example, the "second death" is mentioned (Rev 2:11; 20:14), which refers to eternal death. Referring to death in another sense, Paul writes to the Ephesians that they were "dead in trespasses" before their conversion (Eph 2:5), while they were definitely physically alive at that time. They were thus dead in a figurative sense: spiritually dead in that they were deeply estranged from their Creator. In Genesis 2 and 3 too, this emphasis on spiritual alienation is palpable. This is evident from the fearing of God, and the shame for each other that Adam and Eve have immediately after their sinful act.

Yet, it would go too far to say that in Genesis 3 only this spiritual death is a result of sin, and that our physical death is completely separate from this and would have occurred regardless. For this physical death is definitely the final event in the whole process of our alienation from God, from each other, and from our natural environment. The sinful life that we began to live, as the first chapters of Genesis show, is not sustainable and cannot have a future. In Romans 5 too, it is abundantly clear that physical death is being spoken of. For Paul has just finished speaking about the death of Christ (vv. 8–10), and he obviously had in mind here Christ's exceedingly painful death on the cross. It would not be logical to think that two verses later he would have a totally different death in mind.

In the interpretation of Romans 5:12, we will therefore have to think in a different direction, one that is in line with what we are told in Genesis 2 and 3. In fact, nothing in the Genesis text says that human beings are created as immortal beings. On the contrary, humans were taken from the dust of the earth, and that is an unmistakable sign of their mortality (Gen 3:19b; Ps 103:14–16). The human spirit (*nephesh*), too, is no different than that of the animals: according to ancient near Eastern belief it returns to the earth—it is not until the time of Ecclesiastes that this belief is doubted (Eccl 3:19–21; verse 21: "Who knows whether the human spirit goes upward and the spirit of animals goes downward to the earth?"). The two people in the garden of Eden could therefore only remain alive by being in constant connection with their Creator and his gifts, and not because they were immortal in themselves.

This dependence upon God is symbolized by the tree of life in the garden of Eden. It is striking that Adam and Eve were not forbidden to eat the fruit of this tree. Was this the reason that the man and the woman could remain alive without aging, and could thus avoid death? Or did this tree function as a gateway to eternal life? In any case, it is significant that the human couple is denied access to the tree of life after their sin. From now on they are absolutely prevented from eating its fruit. As a result, human beings will now die at some point, just like the animals.

In this way, it is possible to do justice to what Paul writes about the connection between our sin and our death. That we, humans, are mortal is part of our lives; this is how we've been created. But death was not part of that existence initially. God made sure, so to speak, that death did not have its effect as long as Adam and Eve continued to trust and obey him. It was only when they chose to act for themselves that (ironically!) they could no longer avoid death. It is not without reason, therefore, that we experience death as a curse today, as something that should not really exist. One reason we see it as a curse is because death breaks the bond between people—including the bond between loving partners. We sense that this was not the way things were meant to be from the beginning. It was sin that caused it to be this way. At the same time, full justice can be done in this way to the bare data that have been established by scientific research: like all other organisms humans are subject to death. Aging processes have their effects on us. And because God does not slow those processes or stop them, we go the way of all flesh at some point.

Sin and the Struggle for Existence

Some see yet another conflict between faith and science when it comes to the connection between sin, guilt, and death that Paul makes in Romans 5. They suggest that if human beings emerged from the animal kingdom (and we already saw that there is much evidence that this is the case), it is very unlikely that sin did not occur until the first humans came on the scene. Not only death, but also sin must have been there before them, in the realm of the hominins. For the struggle for life that had raged on earth for countless years must increasingly have been paired with numerous shocking expressions of behavior. All kinds of predators—not only the large ones but also the small—are constantly urged by their aggressions, and hunger, to devour their prey. Within species, competition also drives aggression, and this can be rather violent. Males and females try to secure their own position by eliminating their competitors, or by raising as many strong offspring as they can with the fittest partners they can find. This will also have been the case among the hominins. For them too, it was a case of kill or be killed. So it is inevitable that the first humans must have been born with the same defense and aggression mechanisms, the same urges and tendencies towards violence and promiscuity. In short, could Adam and Eve help it that they sinned? Wasn't that just built into their genes?

In this connection, as we have seen already, Paul makes a thought-provoking comment in Romans 5:13. He makes a distinction between people who know the law and to whom sin is therefore imputed, and those for whom that is not the case. Of course, he did not think of the "problem" we just mentioned, but what he writes is nevertheless applicable to it. Sinful and selfish behavior can only be *accounted* to people when there are clear rules that are broken. Thus, there must also be a certain awareness and understanding of those rules. Such awareness (of such a rule as "I may not kill") is not there in animals, not even in "higher" animal species or most of the hominins. They possessed a body similar to ours but their consciousness was not developed far enough to have knowledge of good and evil, or knowledge of God's covenant that should be kept. And it is precisely this sort of moral knowledge that is addressed in Genesis 2 and 3. Opinions vary on how exactly the relevant texts (Gen 2:17; 3:5, 22) should be interpreted, but this turns out to be the big game-changer: the awareness of good and evil. In particular, it is when the human being obtains experiential knowledge of the difference between good and evil (because of his first evil choices) that things start to go wrong. Indeed, the Hebrew word for "knowledge" does not refer to theoretical knowledge but to practical knowledge, based on one's actual experience.

We humans are, indeed, the first and only creatures among all species, that are able to not be led purely by our urges and instincts. Sometimes we manage to overcome them, and we can consciously make choices that do not harm others. God frequently tells us to do that in the Bible, and he has fully equipped us for it. Perhaps that is why he appointed us to be stewards over creation. God then rightly holds us accountable if we don't make such good choices but remain in the domain of our natural urges or fall back to them. In this way we break the covenant that God established with us. *That is our sin according to Genesis*—and we are held accountable for it because it is our choice, over against God's calling. The story of our fall into sin shows that the first human, Adam, made a choice for himself, with all its consequences: in Adam's slipstream we all chose evil and became addicted to it. But now that Christ has come to free us from that guilt and addiction, it comes down to us to no longer being led by the flesh but by his Spirit. How that is possible, and what such a life looks like, is discussed in detail by Paul in the subsequent chapters of his letter.

Questions for Discussion

1. In this chapter a clear distinction is made between human beings and animals. To what extent is that convincing? Don't humans physically have a similar "building plan" as other mammals? What actually makes us humans unique? In this context, discuss the increased moral status of animals in contemporary opinion-making. Is this development something to be thankful for or does it, in fact, raise questions?

2. Ever since Augustine the church has known the doctrine of so-called *original sin*. What does it consist of? Do you see a basis for it in Romans 5:12, or not? Even if you may find a phrase like "original sin" troublesome, discuss whether there isn't a grain of truth in the underlying thought—and if so, what that grain of truth means for you.

3. To what extent has the fall into sin had negative consequences for our environment? In this context, also read Isaiah 24:4–6 and include that in your discussion.

4. What is your view of human death? Do you see it as severe punishment by God of our sins, is death in your view part of life, or do you see it in yet another way?

Group Activity

Many Christians see the centuries-long struggle for existence, and the sea of suffering and death that it causes in the animal world, as the most difficult problem with which the Christian faith is confronted. In order to deal with this topic from a faith viewpoint, at least four different "solutions" have been proposed:

1. Animals don't experience pain as we humans do—after all, they have a much lower level of consciousness—so there is hardly a problem.

2. The fall has cast its shadow ahead in time. God knew that human beings were going to mess it up, and has therefore "subjected creation to futility" (Rom 8:20) from its very beginning.

3. The constant "killing and be killed" that occurs in the animal world is a result of the demonic forces that have come to disrupt God's good creation. This may have begun before humans came into the world (2 Pet 2:4; Jude 6).

4. God himself planned it this way, and he will also turn it to a good outcome. We must do more than think sentimental thoughts about him and must not want to judge him. It comes down to us trusting him, even when we do not understand his ways.

Give each of these views a number from 1 to 5 (totally disagree—disagree—don't know—agree—totally agree). Explain your view, perhaps in smaller groups. Do you see any other possibilities than the ones mentioned here? Are some combinations possible?

7

To Be Continued

IN CHAPTERS 3–6 WE looked to the past, to the creation of the universe and humankind, and to the origin of sin and evil. In chapter 6 we also discussed the grace that Jesus Christ brought into the world and that is determinative for the present, for our faith and life today. In this chapter we are going shift the direction of our view further, by looking to the future. Here too, we take our point of departure from the Bible, but we also look aside to what science will have to say—in this case about the *future*. Scientists discuss the impending solar death that will inevitably mean the end of all life on earth, to be followed by a Big Freeze (deadly continued expansion) or a Big Crunch (implosion) of the universe. The Bible speaks about the resurrection of the dead followed by eternal life. Are these scenarios mutually exclusive or are they compatible?

Read: 1 Corinthians 15:35–49

Resurrection and Science

One of the most striking differences between believers and secular people is their vision of the future. Secular people typically believe that this life is all there is. Dead is dead. Our ordinary, natural body is all we have, and we certainly should not have any illusions about "pie in the sky when you die," as American activist Joe Hill sang in 1911 (in a parody of a Salvation Army song). There is nothing sweet waiting for us in the sky when we die.

72

We just dissolve into nothing. Or, more accurately, the atoms that our body consist of will be reused in all kinds of ways. Believers, on the other hand, insist that after this life there is a future with God for those who belong to God. This belief is not just held by Christians but by believers of many other traditions as well (for example, by Muslims).

Belief and unbelief are, therefore, diametrically opposed when it comes to how we think about the future. And who is right makes a big difference, of course. For one can hardly think of a greater difference than between disappearing into nothingness and passing into eternal life. You would expect, therefore, that numerous people would want to study theology or philosophy to discover which of the two views has the best evidence to support it. If there are great interests at stake anywhere, then it is here. At the very least, we might be curious to examine the reasons that people have for believing in an eternal future with God.

In the case of the Christian faith, those reasons are clear. Christians believe in an eternal future on the basis of the resurrection of Jesus Christ from the dead. Or, to put it more scientifically, on the basis of what is described in their oldest sources about that event. Of course, one can wonder about the reliability of these reports about Jesus' resurrection in the Gospels and epistles of the New Testament. It has been widely discussed over the last twenty centuries. Believing scholars who have written about the topic, such as Wolfhart Pannenberg and N. T. Wright, hold the messages to be very reliable; their non-Christian colleagues tend to be much more skeptical, even though they fail to come up with a widely agreed-upon alternative explanation. Thus it seems that when it comes to reports about the resurrection, faith and science are completely at odds with each other and a neutral approach is impossible. This is typical for the gospel; Jesus already predicted (Mark 9:40) that you can either be for or against the gospel message, and there is no intermediate position.

Is such a thing as a resurrection from the dead scientifically possible? The very idea is often thought to be ridiculous. Of course not—no one has ever come back! But in science it has often been important to avoid "tunnel vision." It was particularly in the history of science that things that were long considered to be impossible (such as people walking around on the moon) sometimes turned out to be possible after all. Nor can it be said that something which has never been observed before could never happen. With the resurrection we could be dealing with a so-called anomaly, that is a strange event or phenomenon that cannot be explained by current theories but that cannot be dismissed outright either. Such anomalies have often been crucial in the history of science because they have proved to be the harbinger of an important breakthrough to a new understanding (a so-called "paradigm shift"; in our last Bible study we will discuss this concept in more detail). In this way, theologians do indeed interpret the resurrection as the break-through of an entirely new creation. After all, the biblical reports of Jesus' resurrection do not describe the coming alive of a corpse, but the beginning of a totally new way of being—one that is no longer susceptible to illness, aging, and death. Apparently, this new way of being includes new laws of nature that make that existence possible (just as when life arose on earth, new—that is biological—laws of nature became operational).

Two Kinds of Embodiment

In the second part of 1 Corinthians 15 (from verse 12 on, to be precise) Paul does make connections between the resurrection of Jesus, of which he has become totally convinced, and the resurrection of believers at the end of history. He compares the new way of being that begins then with our present existence. It's extremely fascinating to see how he does this and what differences he sees.

This is what Paul says. There are two kinds of bodies, a natural, earthly, body, and a spiritual body (v. 44). In Greek it states a psychic (literally soul-ish) and a pneumatic (spirit-ish, or spiritual) body. With the first, Paul is thinking of the body that we now have—so of what is often called our "nat-ural body." We must not think too negatively about that. As we already saw, the Creator did not produce junk when he made us appear on the earth. To the contrary. Our present body can be compared to a metropolis, fully equipped: houses and factories (our tissues and organs), a city hall where rules are issued (the brain), a police force for the defense against hazardous substances (white blood cells), various transportation and communica-tion systems (nerves and blood vessels), a power plant (heart and lungs), a cleaning system (the kidneys), a garbage collection service, and so on. Our body consists of more than three hundred different kinds of cells, each of which has its own function. All these systems are constantly at work, 24/7, while we are hardly aware of it. If you could look at it with a microscope, what's happening would make you dizzy; all this is going on while you are resting in a chair. Our bodies are unbelievably complex systems. Experts are, therefore, not surprised that people get sick regularly, but, instead, that things can go well for decades and that many people hardly ever get sick. God indeed made us "very good" (Gen 1:31).

And yet, the spiritual body turns out to be even more beautiful. More stable, especially. Only that body is really perfect, so to speak! (We already saw that "very good" in the Bible is not the same as "perfect.") In the passage preceding verse 44, Paul mentioned three things that indicate the differences:

	Natural body	Spiritual body	
1	Perishability	Imperishability	v. 42
2	Dishonor	Glory	v. 43a
3	Weakness	Power	v. 43b

Let's first zoom in a bit on our natural body. It is, to start, perishable. To put it simply, it's going to fail at some point. The mortality is baked in, as it were. And as we get older, our body declines further and further in many different ways. From about our twentieth year of life, it slowly begins to degenerate. That is the dishonor that Paul mentions as his second point. Indeed, what a loss of honor we see when people in their last phase of life gradually lose more bodily and even mental functions. Until, finally, we see a body that is skin and bones. Then you certainly feel what it means that the body will be "sown in dishonor." In the third place, Paul tells us that our present body is "weak." He uses a word here which means that it is susceptible to disease. That, too, is not saying too much. We are constantly at risk of getting cancer, ALS, or whatever disease it may be. Despite all the medical advances, we are often powerless. The natural body is a pitiful body, at times. You can end up in a wheelchair at any time, or worse. The body is thoroughly vulnerable.

The Natural Body as a Creation

The question is unavoidable: how did this come to be this way? For the why question is never far away when we think about illness, aging, and death. And, as we know, the answers to it often come readily too. The dogmatician in me shouts, "That's because of sin! It's our own fault that our bodies have become so vulnerable. If only we hadn't separated ourselves from God in paradise . . ." Remarkably, however, Paul says something else. It's because of the way we've been created, he says. We often miss it when we read it, but Paul consistently emphasizes that it's God who gives every object or creature its own material form (vv. 38–39). In the case of humans, their mortality results from the fact that they are taken from the earth (v. 47, Gen 3:19). That was the case for the first human beings and it holds for all of us. For we all bear the image of the first human being (v. 49). So our bodies are like the one Adam was created with. It is noteworthy that when Paul cites a Bible text to support his view, he does not mention Genesis 3 (the chapter about the fall into sin), but Genesis 2, the chapter about the creation of humans: "The first man became a living being" (Paul adds "first" for the sake of clarity to Genesis 2:7).

That we humans must die at some time is a result of sin, as we saw in the previous chapter on the basis of Romans 5. But from the very beginning we share our *vulnerability* with everything that has been made from matter, that is from the dust of the earth. In no way does Paul suggest that the workings of our bodies would have been altered by the fall. On the contrary, he knows only two kinds of bodily existence: our present natural body, which is transient, and our future spiritual body. So he emphasizes the transience of our present body with the citation from Genesis 2. Life was breathed into our bodies, and so we became "a living being" (for "being," Paul uses the word *psyche*, the common translation of the Hebrew *nephesh*). However, we continue to be vulnerable, for the breath of life can just leave us again, and then all that remains is dust. Just as a church organ falls into disrepair when air is not regularly blown through the pipes, so breath must constantly be taken into our bodies. In the ongoing struggle for existence, our body needs constant maintenance. For we cannot go very long without food and drink, and even shorter without oxygen. Our existence is, therefore, threatened from its beginning and needs constant protection. The biblical view of our human existence and the theory of evolution coincide on this point and complement each other.

The Spiritual Body as a Re-Creation

Later, Paul says, all of this is going to be different. For God's creating work is not finished yet. In Corinth, a striking number of people were sick at the time (1 Cor 11:30). And now Paul says to them, and to the relatives of those who have already died: you may know that another body is waiting for you. That body will no longer start to deteriorate, and that body will also no longer be susceptible to diseases, but will, instead, be sustainable, powerful, and glorious. With "spiritual body," Paul is probably thinking of a body that will be led and directed by the Holy Spirit, and that is, therefore, much more powerful and stable than our present body. It is difficult for us to imagine this new form of embodiment: no worn vertebrae, no lung diseases, no unbearable psychological suffering, no migraines . . .

When you are thinking about that, the question immediately arises: isn't that wishful thinking, or pie in the sky? Paul denies that. There is a physical body, so why can't there be a spiritual one? God is not tied to one concept, is he? God can do things in a totally different way. In the Bible, which is characteristic for that book, things can always be entirely different. They are never tied to one way (to see that, read Ezekiel 18). Many firsts can just become last, and vice versa. To be honest, I think that science actually confirms this changeability of things. There are so many possibilities that lie hidden in creation. Mass can be converted to energy. Life is founded on bits of information. Time proves to be relative, and black holes have their secrets. Things can always be configured differently from what we are accustomed to. It may be that there is even extraterrestrial life, as is now often speculated. Indeed, who can say what is physically possible? From a theological point of view, the resurrection of the dead is no more difficult for God than the creation of the universe. When you have difficulty with the faith, don't let those difficulties start with the article about the resurrection of the dead in the Apostle's Creed; they should start earlier when the creed says "I believe in God the Father Almighty, Maker of heaven and earth." When you can profess those words, the rest of the creed is not so difficult anymore.

You could say that Paul describes his own developmental—or if you wish, evolutionary—theory here: first there is the natural, he says, and then comes the spiritual (v. 46). God apparently works from the less to the more complex, or from the very good to the perfect. His creating work was not yet completed with the creation of the first Adam. For there will also be a re-creation. As we saw, our present body is, even now, very intricate and refined, but the spiritual body shall work even better with its new surroundings. This new condition, which is much more stable and powerful than the previous one, was evidently what God had in mind from the beginning. So it's not the case that Christians (like Neoplatonists) expect some sort of a return to the original state. The Bible in a nutshell is not: "God created humans, these humans spoiled it all, but fortunately Jesus came and therefore everything became as it was again." Rather, God has an original plan (an "eternal counsel," the old theologians called it), and he maintains that plan, whatever happens. Right through human sin and death God realizes his kingdom and creates the new world that he had envisioned from the outset.

The Foundation of Paul's Expectations

It is important to see that Paul does not allow himself to be carried away by his imagination as he writes these things, but that he bases his views solidly on Easter. To put it in theological language: he derives his eschatology strictly from Christology. That is apparent from the piece of text he adds to Genesis 2:7 in verse 45: ". . . the last Adam became a life-giving spirit." He is speaking about Christ here. In the verses that follow, too, Paul makes it clear that everything he writes about the future of human beings is derived from Christ, "the last Adam" in whom all believers are included. As Christ was after Easter, so shall we also be (vv. 48–49). The spiritual body, about which Paul can only stammer, will be like the renewed body of the risen Lord. In his resurrection, Jesus received his body back—but in a renewed state. As a result, the life force does not continually threaten to fall away from him, as it did with Adam and does with us, but instead, flows from him to others. The stream of life has turned around as it were, as the flow of the Chicago River was turned around by civil engineers in 1900. Thus, the second Adam has become a life-giving spirit, who awakens that same new life in those who are connected to him. All who are linked in with Christ will share in his new way of being. Just as we are now all defined by Adam I, we will later become conformed to Adam II.

Paul's expectations are thus not grabbed out of the blue but have a firm foundation. They are, so to say, empirically grounded. They come from what he experienced when he, contrary to all his expectations, met the risen Christ on the road to Damascus (Acts 9). He then also had started to experience the life-giving power that emanated from Christ. So that power is not something that comes later; it's something that's already given now. The Spirit that will soon be leading us into the new mode of existence, it becomes available via Christ already now, in the old way of being.

It's not unlike a story Henri Nouwen tells about a brother and sister who are in the womb of their mother. The little girl believes that there is another life beyond the one in the dark place in which they find themselves. The little boy doesn't believe any of that. He asks, how is life possible without an umbilical cord? The girl responds: But don't you hear the heart that is beating? I believe that is the heart of our mother; she is preparing to bring us into that new life—a life of light and space. Her brother doesn't want to hear any of that. Have you ever seen that so-called mother? he asks skeptically. No, says his sister, but don't you feel those contractions—don't you feel that we're going toward a new life? So here and now, we are already involved in that new life.

The Future of the Cosmos

Meanwhile, the future prospects that Paul sketches here do raise some questions. I mention two: first a scientific one, then a theological one. The scientific question is this: does the expectation of such an eternal way of living in a glorified body agree with the predictions of science about the future of the universe? We already saw that those predictions are really not very rosy. Three possibilities have been suggested, none of them very attractive:

- An ongoing expansion of the universe, in which the temperatures will gradually become lower and lower, so that we will eventually die of a "cold death."

- A moment where the end of the expansion is reached and the opposite movement begins (like a rubber band that returns to its former shape) and we head for a great collapse of the universe under ever higher temperatures ("heat death").

- A back-and-forth movement of the universe between expansion and contraction.

In all three of these scenarios, the sun—and therefore our planet—will have disappeared from the scene much earlier.

At first sight, all three scenarios seem to be at odds with Paul's vision. But here, too, the Christian faith takes into account the almighty power of God. This means that the three scenarios are possible, but only if God allows them to occur. And the latter is not certain. On the contrary: when we keep in mind God's power it is quite possible that he will bring about the transition to the new way of being long before the predicted end of the universe occurs. Paul and other witnesses of the first hour expected this renewal when the Lord returns; they did so on the basis of their meetings with the risen Lord. If God determined the moment when the universe came into being, it is also up to him to determine when and how it will end. So the scenarios for the future as posited by science can remain in place, as long as we take the possibility into account that God may bring into fulfilment his promise of a new heaven and a new earth at an earlier stage. Even here, science and faith are not mutually exclusive.

Why Such a Detour?

The second, theological question is much more difficult: why didn't God create, right from the start, this new spiritual mode of existence that he promised? Why such an enormously long detour with all the suffering and pain that go along with it? We don't know the answer to that question. We'll have to trust that God has his reasons that we do not know about—and we also have good reasons for such trust, given the love towards us that God has shown in his son, Jesus Christ. Augustine already said about this question: apparently God thought it better to bring forth good out of evil than not to allow evil to occur. That was sufficient for Augustine.

Paul suggests in verse 46, however, that there may be a kind of logic in the "stepwise" method of the Creator. Could it be, perhaps, that this long road was especially needed for us humans, for example, to make us immune to sin? Once you have experienced how much misery sin causes and you repent of it (repenting of your own iniquity is a very biblical practice), you shall at some point no longer want it—and thus will no longer want to destroy God's good creation. As a result, the scenario feared by the church father Origen, namely, that on the new earth a new fall into sin could again take place, cannot come to pass. In any case God did not want to make us into robots that automatically do the right thing; instead, God wants us to be people who have to learn to choose the good themselves and become more and more steadfast in doing this. The Dutch theologian A. A. van Ruler (1908–1970) surmised that God had chosen the detour in history to make us humans "fireproof." In any case, when we endorse Paul's words on 1 Corinthians 15, we don't have to be afraid that we are doing something that we should be ashamed of because it is now scientifically outdated or something. Like Paul, we may believe on the basis of the resurrection accounts, that there is—no matter how unimaginable that may be—a new and eternal life awaiting everyone who is in Christ Jesus.

Long ago, there was a British Christian who died poor. He did not leave enough money to have a beautiful text inscribed on his tombstone. Shortly before his death he calculated that he had just enough money for three letters. Those were indeed put on the stone: a "t," a "b," and a "c." The abbreviation for "to be continued." A perfect choice. For indeed, our life will be continued—thanks to him who will change our tarnished body so that it will become conformed to his glorious body, according to the power with which he can subject all things to himself (Phil 3:21).

Questions for Discussion

1. Do you find it difficult (at times) to believe in the resurrection of Jesus? If so, does that have to do with modern science, with the skepticism about the resurrection from the dead that has always been around, even long before the emergence of modern science (see Acts 17:32, for example)? Or do you have yet another reason?

2. In this Bible study it is suggested that there is often more agreement between the Christian faith and evolutionary theory than is often thought. What do you think of this? What do you see as the greatest problem with which the theory of evolution confronts the believer? And, conversely, what could be some meaningful ideas that the Christian faith offers above and beyond the basic evolution theory?

3. This chapter deals especially with the resurrection of the dead at the end of time. How do you imagine the so-called "intermediate state"— that is, the time between the moment a believer dies and the moment when the resurrection of the dead will take place?

4. Discuss the differences between our present-day body and the powerful resurrection body. To what extent can Paul's words comfort us, perhaps at times when we may be constantly struggling with our body's illnesses or handicaps?

5. "Christians do not expect a return to an original state but a transition to a much more stable existence than there ever was before." Talk about this statement. To what extent is it of missional importance—or to put it in a different way: to what extent is this something that we can discuss in an inviting and meaningful way with secular neighbors or colleagues?

Group Activity

Use an internet search engine, for ten minutes, to find information about "transhumanism." Tell each other what you have found and what you think transhumanism means. Keep it as factual as possible. How realistic, do you think, is the scenario that human beings can use robotics and new information technologies to begin to lead a superhuman existence? After this discussion of facts, go around on this subject a second time, telling each other what feelings this philosophy invokes in each of you. How do you feel about the fact that people put their hopes in this? Do you see connections to the biblical message (think of Gen 6:1–6 or Gen 11:4, for example)?

8

Convincing Proof?

"Not enough evidence, God!" That's what the British philosopher, Bertrand Russell (1872–1970) said he would answer God upon his death when God would ask him why he had not believed in him. Not enough convincing proof. This is still a reason for many to keep their distance from anything that has to do with God, faith, and church. If God really wants me to believe in him, they say, then he should give an irrefutable proof of his existence. If God is almighty, that shouldn't be too difficult for him. Believers, too, can suffer from the hiddenness of God, and long for God to become more evident in their lives. We meet such a believer in the Gospel of John.

Read: John 14:1–11

Philip as Empiricist

To be sure, John 14 is not about whether there is enough evidence for the existence of God, for that was not in question for the disciples. Doubt about the existence of God is of a much later date, and occurs mainly in the West. However, Jesus' unexpected announcement of his imminent departure had created great uncertainty among the disciples. They are very confused about this. Where would their rabbi be going, precisely? And why couldn't they come along (13:36)? It all sounded so threatening. So their hearts were troubled, anxious, and deeply worried (14:1). But Jesus calls them to have trust in God and in himself. Don't be afraid; it's going to turn out well! Along with all of this, Jesus lets them know once again how intimately he is connected with his heavenly Father. He prepares a way for his students to the Father. In this way he is, himself, the way. He is also the truth—that is, the trustworthy one, who does what he says. And for this reason, he's also life. For in God, the real life is to be found. In fact, he and the Father are one. So if you were to really know me, he states, you would also know my Father. And then he enigmatically continues: "From now on you do know him and have seen him."

At that moment, it's all too much for one of Jesus' students, a man called Philip. He calls out, "Lord, show us the Father, and we will be satisfied" (v. 8). Then you don't need any more words and speeches. We sense a certain amount of irritation behind Philip's exclamation. His rabbi can say all kinds of beautiful words, and he does so extensively in the Gospel of John, but it would be much more convincing if he came up with some *proof*. Earlier in the Gospel of John, Philip had shown himself to be someone who tends toward empiricism, toward what can be established by evidence. In chapter 1, for example, his friend Nathanael reacts rather skeptically to Philip's announcement that he has discovered the Messiah in a certain Jesus from Nazareth. Can something special come from such an obscure town that is never mentioned by the prophets? It is striking that Philip does not enter into a debate about this. He does not initiate a big theological argument that would prove that there is nothing wrong with Nazareth as a possible hometown of the Messiah. Instead, he simply says, "Come and see for yourself." Or even more succinctly, "Come and see." Convince yourself on the basis of the empirical data. This data, according to Philip—and later also according to Nathanael—did not really allow any other possible explanation.

The second time Philip makes a comment in the Gospel of John, he is again an empiricist and, in that sense, a realist. In John 6:5, Jesus asks Philip where they can buy bread to feed the large crowd that has come to see Jesus. Philip, who came from the surrounding area, then makes a rapid estimation of the size of the crowd and multiplies that by the cost of a simple meal of bread. His conclusion is that even if they had 200 denarii—that is 200 times the amount that a laborer would be paid for a hard day's work—they would still not be able to supply all the people present with even a small piece of bread. He thus makes a realistic calculation and, on that basis—we would say in a scientifically responsible way—he concludes that the plan of his master is unworkable. But Jesus, the Gospel writer adds, has deliberately burdened Philip with this problem, in order to test him. In other words, to see whether he was able to look at this problem through the eyes of faith. In that case, Philip might have relied on previous events he had experienced with Jesus (e.g., at the wedding in Cana, John 2:1–11) and come to a different conclusion.

In chapter 14, too, Philip still seems to favor empirical evidence. What Jesus tells him is not enough. On the other hand, what Jesus can present as visible evidence *is* convincing for him. You could say that Philip shows a kind of scientific mindset, and applies it, as it were, to faith. It is remarkable that he does so long before our scientific age. Apparently, we should not be too quick to see present-day science as the great culprit and enemy of faith. In a world where there is still no such thing as experimental science, Philip already shows a critical-realistic attitude that leads him to a certain skepticism. This seems to be an ageless attitude. All the more reason to pay close attention to how Jesus deals with this. But before we continue to discuss this, we first need to have a brief discussion of contemporary science.

Respect for the Facts

In scientific research, the visible and measurable reality is indeed very important. This is for a very good reason: it's the only way we can find out how things are put together and how they work. It took quite a long time before scientists dared to let go of their own ideas about how nature *must* be put together and to let nature speak for itself. "Don't think, look!" is a well-known motto in science these days. Look as carefully as you can and let what you see determine what you think. In this way, the Christian astronomer Johannes Kepler (1571–1630) could be the first to demonstrate the correctness of Copernicanism (i.e., the theory that the earth and other planets orbited around the sun)—even though he had to use a lot of complex mathematical calculations to do so. Furthermore, Kepler dared to let go of the ancient and generally accepted idea that the planetary orbits should be circular. That view was not in agreement with the observations, and he had become weary to accept all the makeshift modifications to the theory to "save" the circularity of the orbits. If we take the empirical approach and place trust in our sensory observations, Kepler reasoned, then we can conclude that the planetary orbits are not circular but elliptical. At the time it sounded almost sacrilegious because the planetary orbits were circular according to a long and venerable philosophical tradition—Plato and his perfect circles continued to have much influence. However, Kepler's idea made the pieces of the puzzle fall precisely into place. From that moment, Copernicanism would definitely win the battle.

Admittedly, things are often more complex than the simple motto "don't think, look!" suggests, since what we see when we look is to some extent co-determined by what we think—a phenomenon that is known as the "theory-ladenness of observation." Yet, this does not mean that we can continue to see only what we want to see without repercussions. At the end of the day, the empirical world can "talk back", and this is precisely what science is looking for. Think for example of the way vaccines are developed and tested (I write these lines only a short time after the COVID crisis). Time and again, reality will have its say. Hence, we see all kinds of trials, double-blind studies with control groups, and so on, all to find out as precisely as possible how viruses react to our interventions. That's why scientists should avoid saying more than their research findings allow, and should not jump to conclusions that are not empirically based. Thoughtful scientists will not come with nice-sounding one-liners and sweeping statements, but will express themselves carefully—and may even sound boring doing so. Such modesty is to their credit. We can even discern in it a form of respect towards the Creator—implicitly, of course, because not all of them are believers. They are afraid, as they should be, to project their own ideas upon reality and to declare them to be true, for that turned out to be a mistake so often in the past. Only the path of careful research, of experiments and observations time and again, of calculating, checking and double-checking, turned out to take us further and further in knowing reality, in fighting diseases, in developing new agricultural technology, etc. From that point of view, Philip's empiricism was a good attitude to have.

Not only natural scientists but many social scientists (such as psychologists, economists, and sociologists) today also try to work with empirical methods as much as possible. They make every effort to adopt the methodologies of the "hard sciences." Whereas in the past people were impressed by the psychological theories of someone like Sigmund Freud, today they are considered to be largely obsolete because they cannot be experimentally verified in any way. What social scientists propose must be able to withstand questioning, and must thus be based on "measurement." Using qualitative methods (such as interviews) and quantitative research (such as broadly based surveys) investigators attempt to find all kinds of connections and patterns. Sometimes this approach fails, when, for example, data are tampered with to please a client or to boost one's own reputation. But it is telling that when such a thing comes to light, a major scandal is the direct result, and university administrators do not hesitate to deal harshly with it. In this case, one speaks of the "self-cleansing capacity" of academic research. When results cannot be replicated (= repeated), the scientist will sooner or later be exposed.

Besides the natural and social sciences, there is a third category of academic disciplines: the so-called humanities, which study all kinds of products of the human mind, such as language, literature, art, law, religion, and music. History and archaeology are important disciplines in the humanities; they examine human expressions (writings and other artifacts) from the past. The rules of the game for the humanities have a character all of their own. Interpretation plays a more important role than in the natural and social sciences. And it is difficult to avoid bringing values into the humanities. That is why, for example, *the* definitive history of the Second World War will never be written. There will always be other possible interpretations that can and will be brought forward. This does not mean, however, that anything goes. In the humanities, too, it is generally possible to distinguish between wheat and chaff. Everyone has to play the game fairly, with respect for the empirical facts. This scientific mentality has fundamentally changed the face of the world in many ways.

Can Faith Be Proven?

The burning question is now: what happens when we apply this mentality to the world of faith? It seems that this is what Philip is pushing for. He wants to see evidence. Is that desirable, or do things go off the rails when we look for proof? In any case, it must have been difficult for a person with a rational approach, such as Philip, to make a decision *without* any evidence. And it's not necessarily wrong to look for such evidence. In the great commandment that Jesus cited from the Old Testament, we are called to love the Lord God, not only with our heart and soul, but also with our mind (Mark 12:30). Our minds and intellects do not need to be put aside when we enter the world of church and faith. To the contrary, they can participate fully, and our faith can be greatly clarified and strengthened by our intellect.

Theologians have realized this throughout the centuries. They have regarded themselves as professional scholars and attempted to support and illuminate the existence of God. Many of them still do so today. While it is often said that we cannot prove the existence of God and should not even want to do that, many theologians and other Christian thinkers do put all kinds of *arguments* forward for that they find convincing to a greater or lesser extent. Those interested in this topic can read, for example, *Is There a God?*, by Richard Swinburne (2010), or Robert J. Spitzer's *New Proofs for the Existence of God* (2010). The arguments that one encounters in books such as these are often far from simple; nor are most of them particularly appealing. But the question is, of course, whether they hold water. Usually that cannot be demonstrated in a watertight way. Therefore, most of these authors claim that they provide arguments (the force of which depends on whether one accepts the assumptions) rather than knock-down proofs. They clearly show that these arguments are, in any case, by no means unreasonable, and that is quite an important observation. In our society there is an unspoken sentiment that you are a bit behind the times when you "still" (nasty little word!) believe in God. As if to say that we all know much better nowadays. But that is more related to the spirit of the times than it is based on the content of the belief. In any case, thus far all attempts to show that God does *not* exist have failed.

Suffice it to say that faith in God is not doomed to failure as soon as you start to look at it in a scholarly responsible, academic way. Nor should we be afraid of that. The Christian faith can withstand a knock or two. *For it has, itself, an empirical basis.* That is, its basis is what once actually happened in the history of salvation. Even when the Bible looks at events from a very specific perspective, and may exaggerate at times—for example when it comes to large numbers; exaggeration was used at the time when you wanted to make a point perfectly clear—then the main idea of the narrative can nevertheless withstand pointed questioning (see, for example Luke 1:1–4; 1 Cor 15:6). That four Gospels differ from each other in details but broadly agree with each other speaks volumes in this regard. In other parts of the Bible too, such as the Old Testament, we constantly see references to concrete events (such as the passage through the Red Sea) and we become aware of what experiences, reactions, and expectations they evoked. We then properly speak of the trustworthiness and inerrancy of the Bible and do not look for that in all kinds of details but in its overall story lines, its common thread.

Thus, if someone were to ask you to lay proof of the faith on the table ("Show us the Father!"), the best answer would be to invite that person to begin to read the Bible. For in the biblical witness of what happened then, there, in and around Israel, the empirical basis of the Christian faith can be found. That is why honest research of the Bible is so important. Because, as the twentieth century theologian Hendrikus Berkhof once said, "salvation hinges on history"—that is, on the history that is told in the Bible.

Two Kinds of Knowledge

Yet, rarely will anyone come to the faith on the basis of philosophical arguments or historical research. In fact, when this does happen at all, this faith—particularly at the beginning—may be a rather distant belief. This has sometimes been called a "historical faith," since it is centered on the bare conviction that God exists and that what is written in the Bible is generally correct in a historical sense. Some may even boast that they believe the Bible "from cover to cover," as if that is an extraordinary achievement. "And if it were written in the Bible that Jonah swallowed the big fish instead of the other way around, I would have believed that too," someone once added defiantly. But remarkably, the Bible does not have a high regard for such historical knowledge in and of itself. The demons also believe that God exists, we read, but they don't benefit from that; to the contrary, it only makes them afraid of him—they shudder (Jas 2:19). Such a belief in the factual correctness of religious opinions doesn't get you any further, because it doesn't change your life.

When the Bible deals with believing in, and knowing, God, it usually means something different or, in any case, it means much more. Then it is not about the bare conviction that God exists, but about a warm, personal connection to God. We find this, for example, in Psalm 25, where it is written: "The friendship of the Lord is for those who fear him" (vs. 14). We nourish this friendship, this intimate communion with God in prayer, Scripture reading, and contemplation in which we experience God's care and love. We can "take it to the Lord in prayer." The knowledge that we gain in such a personal relationship is of a different nature than objective, scientific knowledge. In the theory of knowledge (the expensive word is *epistemology*) we can, as we saw in the first Bible study, distinguish between various types of knowledge. Leaving aside, for example, moral knowledge, aesthetical knowledge, etc., two important categories are:

1. Factual knowledge, also called "propositional knowledge" (a proposition is a sentence in which a certain fact is stated, for example "this table is purple").

2. Experiential knowledge, also called personal knowledge or relational knowledge.

It will be clear that the two do overlap, but each still has its own characteristics. The way that I know my parents includes my knowing all kinds of facts about them (such as when it is their birthday, where they have lived, and what kinds of work they have done). But experiential knowledge goes beyond factual knowledge. It includes all kinds of personal experiences and involvements that cannot simply be expressed in propositions. But it is precisely that personal aspect, the way I got to know them, that made the difference in my life and that determines my attitude towards them. The most significant thing in this is whether I know my parents cared about me and loved me.

The experiential knowledge that we acquire is, in general, much more important than the propositional knowledge that we have. For it is the personal experiences, and not the facts that we know, that make us into the person we are. They determine our identity and influence our character and our actions. The same is true for the experiences we have with God. In all this, it's not only about certain inner, "mystical" feelings we might have, but also about experiences that you gain as you deal with other people, or through the faith community to which you belong. You are shaped by Word and sacraments, and by prayer and the way in which you have experienced God's guidance in your life. Decisive in this is whether you have encountered God's selfless love. For that love, which became embodied in the flesh and blood of Jesus, forms the center of the biblical message. When that love has touched you, that is decisive. Then you no longer need hard evidence for God's existence ("Show us the Father!"). Then you know him personally, in the way he came to you and loves you. Then you get involved with heart and soul with God—even though he is sometimes far away, and he never becomes ours to possess. As a Dutch hymn has it: "God comes into our life, not as a storm or a flood / but in a dying existence [that is, in the suffering and death of Jesus] he becomes believable for us."

Decisive Faith

With this in mind, we finally pause for a moment at the reaction Jesus gives in John 14 to Philip's exclamation. Philip wanted to have objective proof, so to speak, of Jesus' claims. But Jesus answers him that such proof is not at all necessary: "Have I been with you all this time, Philip, and you still do not know me?" (vs. 9). It is interesting that Philip is explicitly addressed by his name at this moment. Thus, Jesus refers here to the experiential knowledge of Philip, to the personal knowledge that he had gained with Jesus over the years. It disappoints him that Philip apparently did not take those experiences more seriously. What did Philip expect, really, in his request for a theophany, a visual appearance of God? God is a spiritual being, so God cannot even show himself, or he would have to do so by assuming an external form, say, the form of a human being. And isn't that exactly what God has done! That is what the apostle John has emphasized throughout his Gospel: the Word that was with God, and that was God, has become flesh and lived among us (John 1:1, 14). Jesus himself repeatedly said, whoever has seen me has seen the Father. Then it does come down to letting yourself be convinced of that. That is why in this passage Jesus repeatedly calls us to faith, to trust, and to surrender ourselves to him. And even though Jesus himself is no longer physically around, his Spirit has been given us in his place to remind us of him and lead us to faith through his words (John 14:26).

If you are not prepared to have such faith and trust, being confronted with "hard" evidence is not going to help. For evidence is not usually so hard, in the sense of being knock-down. We see that today too, when it comes to science. Numerous skeptics would rather put their trust in fake news, for example with regard to the climate of the earth, than to let themselves be convinced by scientific research. So, you can always avoid the evidence if you wish. That is also the case when it comes to faith (there are indeed remarkable parallels between faith and science). In matters of faith, too, we can speak of good arguments and important historical data that support it. Thus, there are important arguments, open to anyone who wants to investigate them, for the resurrection of Jesus as the best possible explanation for the New Testament reports about it. But these will never be convincing if we don't want to open up our closed frame of mind according to which divine miracles are impossible. To open up one's closed frame of mind means to open up oneself to the living God, who speaks to us through the New Testament. If we don't allow ourselves to be convinced by his word to us, then "neither will [we] be convinced even if someone rises from the dead" (Luke 16:31).

Questions for Discussion

1. Can you relate to Philip's desire for a shortcut—that is, a shortcut to certainty of faith because God would just show himself? In this context, what do you learn from the answer that Jesus gives to Philip and his cohorts? As you think about this, notice how the text speaks about Jesus' abiding care and love for his disciples.

2. Do you see yourself as a person interested in the natural sciences or more interested in the social sciences? Or the humanities? Does that make a difference in how you act and think in daily life? And in your life of faith?

3. Do you think faith in God can be supported by proof? And, more specifically, is that the case for the Christian faith?

4. In the life of the everyday, there are many things we are sure of without having evidence for them. That's because our memory and our senses are basically reliable. According to Calvin and contemporary Christian philosophers, we humans have a "sense for God." When that functions well, we may spontaneously come to faith and it may also give us a basic knowledge of God. What do you think of that idea? If humans have such a sense, then what do we think of people who are not believers? In this connection, also read Romans 1:19–20.

5. We have emphasized the importance of "honest Bible study." Many Christians, on the other hand, are somewhat hesitant about current Bible research and biblical scholarship. Why do you think that is? To what extent do you think these people have a point?

Group Activity

One of the greatest mathematicians and physicists of all times was the brilliant French Christian thinker Blaise Pascal (1623–1662). Among many other things, Pascal thought deeply about the relationship between faith and the evidence for that faith. One of his most famous texts is the so-called

Mémorial, a short manuscript ("Fire") that was found after his death, sown into the lining of his coat. Find this text on the internet, here for example: https://ccel.org/ccel/pascal/memorial/memorial.i.html. Discuss with each other what Pascal's ideas evoke in you and what touches you. Try to make a connection between this and what has been discussed in this Bible study.

9

Risky Philosophy

Several areas of academic study have already been discussed in the previous chapters, but we have not yet dealt with *philosophy* directly, even though it is an enormously important discipline in which much happens that, consciously or unconsciously, shapes our thinking. In the Bible, the word "philosophy" occurs only once, in Colossians 2, the passage that is central to this Bible study. At first glance, it appears that not much good is said about philosophy, for it is seen as a temptation. Indeed, philosophers and their systems of thought have sometimes tempted Christians to adapt the gospel and to transform it into something else. We will therefore consider how this might work today and how we can be on the watch for that. At the same time, it is clear that the writer of the letter to the Colossians has a very specific system of thought in mind and certainly not all philosophy. There's a lot of good to be said about other forms of philosophy, and in this chapter we want to pay some attention to those as well. It can be said that, in general, the church has always sought to be in conversation with influential philosophers. Christians realized that they could learn from them, even if these philosophers themselves were not Christians.

Read: Colossians 2:4–10

Paul, Timothy, and the Letter to the Colossians

We start with a preliminary issue. According to quite a few contemporary Bible scholars, the letter to the Colossians (like some the other epistles labeled Pauline) has not been written by Paul but has its origin in the circle of his pupils. When we are accustomed to accept what such an epistle says about its own authorship, it would seem obvious to dismiss such a theory immediately: Colossians 1:1 states that the letter is written by Paul, so that is the case . . . However, that can be a little short-sighted. We know from antiquity the phenomenon of so-called "pseudepigraphy": an author ascribes his or her writings to another author. This can be seen as a kind of reverse plagiarism: you don't put something that you derive from someone else in your own name, but, instead, you put something that you have written in someone else's name. In our individualistic times, both are seen as something objectionable. Indeed, strictly speaking you may be said to "lie" when you attribute a letter you wrote yourself to someone else, just like you do when you suggest that you are the one who wrote a text that in fact originated with someone else.

At that time, however, pupils of a particular rabbi or philosopher sometimes had so much respect for their master that they didn't write in their own name but only in the name of the master. Compare this to the way in which young painters used to work throughout the centuries, signing their work with their master's name rather than with their own. In these cases one wanted to say: "I don't want to bring forward anything of my own but only the ideas of my master." And readers would typically know that this was the case—it was not a lie but a convention. Yet, of course these pupils wrote and painted in their own style, which sometimes differed quite a bit from that of their master. In the case of some biblical letters, scholars have noticed that their style reflects a somewhat later time period. Careful biblical scholars suspect that in some sense this is the case here, and that the Letter to the Colossians originated in the circle of Paul's pupils. In this case, however, it is conceivable that the (now old) Paul did have input, for example when it comes to personal details that appear in the letter. Colossians 4:18 shows that Paul has only signed the letter, so that the lion's share was thus written by someone else. It is obvious to think here of Timothy, whose name is mentioned in 1:1 together with Paul's (therefore there is no attempt here to hide the identity of the real author). In fact, given 1:1, it seems strange to assume that the letter was written by Paul alone. We might do more justice to what the text actually says! To correct this, we will refer to Timothy as the main author in what follows below.

It is not necessary to take a strong position in the debate about the authorship of this letter. There are also careful New Testament scholars who *do* attribute the Colossians letter to Paul, and they may well be correct in their opinion. What is at stake here is whether we should say on the basis of the Christian faith: "In the Bible, by definition, there cannot be any writings that state they are written by one person and are in fact written by someone else," or that we can leave the discussions on this topic to biblical scholars and can take the results of their debate seriously. We already saw that, at the time, pseudepigraphy was not morally wrong but could, in fact, be seen as being "polite": you don't want to show off feathers that are not your own. If we take that fact as a starting point, then it is not surprising that pseudepigraphic writings can also occur in the Bible. It does not make a difference for the message—for that is not changed by this—and it doesn't change the authority of the Bible either. However, it does become difficult when such an epistle mentions all kinds of personal details, for example about Paul. For we would then have to assume that the author used these details, or even made them up, to create the impression that the author is really Paul and can therefore write with Paul's authority. In the case of the letter to the Colossians we saw that this assumption is not necessary; Paul himself could still have been involved with the epistle. Incidentally, there are quite a few letters that state they are written by Paul, such as those written to the Romans, the Galatians, the first Letter to the Thessalonians, and both letters to the Corinthians, about which biblical scholars almost unanimously agree that they were actually written by Paul himself.

The Colossian Heresy

Throughout the entire letter to the Colossians, Timothy is intent on fighting a certain false doctrine, the so-called "Colossian heresy." However, it is very difficult to get a good insight into the exact contours of this spiritual movement. It *is* clear that this heresy exerted a considerable amount of influence on the Christian community in Colossae and that Timothy, for that reason, took a firm stand against it. It's good to see how in doing so he does not let himself be led by the thinking of his opponents but, rather, chooses a positive approach: he begins with the good news about Jesus Christ as the Colossians had received it from Epaphras (1:7). He describes the significance of this good news in detail. As far as Timothy is concerned, one cannot emphasize the gifts we have in Christ strongly enough. The Colossian believers owe everything to his self-sacrifice on the cross (1:20). And thanks to the worldwide significance of that very same Christ (1:16–18), they also have nothing to fear. For in his resurrection, he has already triumphed over all the powers. They don't need more than him, "in whom are hidden all the treasures of wisdom and knowledge" (2:3). Thus, the Colossians can depend on Christ for all their knowledge of faith and wisdom of life.

It is then vitally important that they actually do that, of course, because only in this way can they have a firm foundation and remain steadfast in the Christian faith (1:23). And precisely on this point Timothy has some concerns. It is in this context that we find his comments about "the philosophy," which he connects with "empty deceit, according to human tradition, according to the elemental spirits of the universe, and not according to Christ" (2:8). What does Timothy mean, exactly? It is clear that his words refer to heretical ideas that he saw gaining influence in Colossae, much to his regret. All kinds of other matters that he mentions in his letter are related to the practices and way of thinking of this movement. Among New Testament scholars, numerous theories circulate about what kind of group, sect, or movement Timothy may have had in mind. They compare the characteristics mentioned in the letter with spiritual writings from the same or preceding times and attempt to make it plausible that there is a connection. But even after twenty centuries there is still no clarity about the actual nature of the group. None of the past and present proposals is fully convincing. What is clear is that the group embodied a mixture of Jewish (concerned as they were with "Sabbaths" and "circumcision," 2:11–16) and gentile religious ideas and practices; but no group of that time has yet been found that incorporates exactly the characteristics mentioned in the letter.

Seductive Philosophy

It is useful to pause to think about our lack of understanding, twenty centuries later, of what Paul and Timothy were thinking of exactly when they wrote the Colossians text we are discussing. In that respect there is a challenging and fascinating task for future biblical scholars who can help us understand this topic more fully. In any case, the research that these scholars carry out is fascinating and exciting! Many people think that theologians and Bible scholars know just about anything there is to know about the

Bible, but that is often not the case. Sometimes we can understand extra-Scriptural references clearly, but we can't in other cases, and even more often, opinions vary. That in itself is not regrettable—the common thread that runs through the epistle is crystal clear, precisely because of its positive approach. But it does keep us humble.

In this regard, you could compare our knowledge of Scriptures with that of the cosmos: through the contributions of scholarship, we have come to know both worlds, the ones of the Bible and the cosmos, better and better, but we have also become more aware of how much we still do not yet know. From this point of view, scholarship does not make us presumptuous but, rather, it leads to humility. This is also the case for biblical studies. At the same time, we can see in this situation an invitation to move, in some small way, the boundaries of our knowledge by way of ongoing research. In this regard, the study of the Bible and the cosmos—let's say biblical theology and astronomy—resemble each other. Like all areas of scholarship, they share this passionate drive to obtain more knowledge than we have at present.

In the meantime, it is striking that Timothy designates the movements that he is opposing as "the philosophy." He emphatically uses the definite article ("the"), so it is not about philosophy in general but about this particular philosophy that, according to him, amounts to a hollow sham. Characteristic is that it is seductive in a particular way and that you can just get sucked into it, away from Christ. That must be due to the "plausible arguments" mentioned in verse 4. These can indeed be used by philosophers—the Greek sophists, for example, were known for their rhetorical reasoning skills with which they could make the crooked straight—and that may well be the reason why the word "philosophy" is used here. At that time, it could refer to any spiritual, religious, or philosophical movement. While today we quickly associate philosophy with "autonomous reason" and sometimes with unbelief, we are dealing here with a thoroughly *religious* movement that leaned heavily on human traditions.

Scientism: Science on a Pedestal

Apart from the question of which system of thought Timothy may have had in mind, we recognize today the image of a philosophy that assumes religious overtones and, by its sheer power of persuasion, can take you into its grip. Many contemporary examples of such philosophies, or views of life, could be mentioned in this connection. In the context of what we are focusing on in this book, however, we will apply Timothy's warning to one such philosophy in particular: that of *scientism*. If you look at the word closely, you notice that the word science is linked to the ending "-ism," which usually indicates the absolutization of a certain point of view. Indeed, we can describe scientism as the absolutization of science and of scientific knowledge. Today, scientism is a very popular philosophical belief. Some thinkers profess and defend it openly, and even see it as their belief; a much greater group of people let themselves unwittingly be influenced by it. Scientism, a deeply rooted trust in science as the enterprise that will always rescue us in time (for example also from our climate problems) is in the air we breathe today. But that trust could lead to disappointment at crucial times.

When we think about this, we realize that this is because the Christian faith used to determine our orientation toward the big questions of life, but that this role is now given to science. Indeed, scientists and other academics seem to have become the new priests of our time. It's assumed that they not only have knowledge of their field but of all kinds of other things as well, even things that have little to do with their field of specialization. Some even pretend to have a monopoly on the "scientific" truth when it comes to questions that science cannot even answer satisfactorily, such as:

- whether people are free to act or whether our freedom to act is an illusion;

- whether objective norms of good and evil exist;

- whether there is more to us than our brain;

- what the meaning is of our lives;

- whether God exists.

The rule that is used in this discussion is that only science can lead to reliable knowledge. Thus, any claim that cannot be defended scientifically (that is, which is not "evidence-based," as it is called), cannot be true—notwithstanding the fact that in everyday life all of us believe many things to be true that have not been proven, and rightly so. This scientism leaves little room for recognizing the things that transcend us and that cannot be adequately addressed in a scientific way. It is noteworthy in this regard that Reformed Epistemology, as it is called, formulated from the 1980s onwards by American philosophers like Alvin Plantinga and Nicholas Wolterstorff, holds that from a philosophical point of view religious belief can be acceptable even if it is not based on arguments or evidence—just like a host of our other beliefs (e.g., the belief that we had breakfast this morning, or that there is a tree in our garden) are not based on arguments or evidence.

In all this, it's understandable how scientism could have arisen. By strictly holding to scientific research methods, we have been able to greatly increase our knowledge of reality. In this way, our abilities to control and work with reality have increased greatly. Just think of the simple—but in its simplicity, iconic—example of the lightning rod. For centuries, countless people died as a result of lightning strikes, which were often attributed to the anger of the gods. That didn't change until Benjamin Franklin discovered experimentally that lightning is actually an electrical discharge, and that it is possible to conduct the energy that is released into the ground. Where for many centuries religious explanations hadn't brought us any further in combating the results of lightning strikes, the scientific explanation did so instantly.

In other areas of study, too, scientific discoveries and explanations have been enormously successful. Just think of medicine. Moreover, there appears to be little difference of opinion about many scientific theories and claims. While there is little agreement about religious statements, everyone—regardless of his or her worldviews—agrees, for example, on the correctness of the laws of Boyle and Gay-Lussac, just to mention an example. From this point of view, it is indeed tempting to think that only scientific knowledge can be taken seriously and that everything that wants to pass for knowledge must be scientifically "validated." You can't do the potential buyer of a particular product a greater favor than by stating that the effectiveness of that product has been "scientifically proven" (the question of what that evidence looks like is often ignored). Thus, the absolutization of scientific knowledge is in the air, and it's easy to be carried away with this scientism in your thinking. The "plausible arguments" (v. 4) that advocate it are usually close at hand. But when it comes to matters of belief, it leaves you little to hold on to, for scientism leads to a cold atheism. If what can be scientifically proven is the only thing that counts, God and faith in God quickly fall by the wayside. Then science replaces trust in God. When this happens, science becomes what is known as an *idol* in the Bible: we put our hope in it and expect our salvation from it—but in vain. For no matter how much science can positively influence our lives, we then still expect too much from it. Our most profound questions about life cannot be answered by science; nor can it bring us to our human destiny, which is to flourish forever as creatures being made in the image of God.

Do Not Distrust Science but This Philosophy

Because some scientists turn science into a kind of ideology in this way, as a reaction many believers have become rather suspicious of anything that is called science. Particularly those who have not directly followed a scientific education themselves can easily come to the conclusion that it is apparently *science* that all too often leads to unbelief. Many people who abandon the faith mention this. Often one can hear stories along the lines of: "As a child I believed in God, but science saw to it that I have left my faith behind." Moreover, this kind of faith-based skepticism towards science is easily strengthened by, and conflated with, the more general distrust vis-à-vis official institutions (the government, the media, the church, etc.) that characterizes large swaths of contemporary Western societies.

It would be a misconception, however, to think that science is in a tense relationship with faith, and that this would be a reason to abandon one of them. Rather, it is a particular *philosophy* that is causing the problem here—the philosophy of scientism. So, it's not science that is the risky enterprise but, as in the days of Timothy and Paul, it's a particular type of philosophy that is the problem. When "plausible arguments" are used to link science to this philosophy, this can lead to the erosion and eventual disappearance of your faith. However, the philosophy of scientism does not appear to be tenable. First of all, it does not do justice to life—for example, not to our ultimate loves and longings, nor to our being profoundly attuned to a relationship with our Creator. It does not do justice to the fact that we cannot live by stark rationality, but need an understanding of life that is greater and more comprehensive, and that places our existence in a meaningful context. Scientism cannot offer any of these things. And second, scientism is even untenable according to its own standards, since it cannot be scientifically verified itself. In fact, science cannot stand on its own feet, since scientific research inevitably relies on sources of knowledge that are nonscientific, such as perception, memory, and common sense. Of course, what emerges from these sources of knowledge must be scientifically tested, but if our common senses were completely unreliable, they would not be able to contribute anything to science. And who is to say that these sources of knowledge are the only ones? Who is to say that human beings cannot also have a sense of the beautiful, the good, and God? This thought brings us to another form of philosophy.

A Non-Reductive Philosophy

While philosophical thinking can thus be tempting and bring you into secular ways of thinking, it would be nonsense to think that this applies to all philosophies. We already saw that, when speaking of "the" (= this particular) philosophy, Timothy realized this too. There's also philosophy that does not absolutize scientific knowledge, but incorporates it in a comprehensive whole and assumes that we human beings, in addition to scientific knowledge, also have other forms of knowledge that may be even more important. A form of philosophy that many Christians (and others besides) find helpful in this regard is the "theory of modal aspects" formulated by the Dutch philosopher Herman Dooyeweerd (1894–1977). Characteristic of this theory is that it attempts to do justice to the diversity of created reality without declaring one aspect to be the only or dominant one. Dooyeweerd rightly claimed that his theory was philosophical rather than theological—that is, one does not need to have a specific faith perspective to see its point, although the Christian faith is certainly conducive to it.

Very concretely, Dooyeweerd proposed that fifteen aspects or ways of being and functioning can be distinguished in reality as we know it. These "modalities" build stepwise upon each other: they each show, so to speak, a new level in reality. It takes us too far afield to work out the details of this theory here, but it is instructive to see which aspects of reality Dooyeweerd was thinking of when he formulated his theory, and with which branches of scholarship they correspond.

	name	*nucleus*	*discipline*
1.	numerical	discrete quantity, number	arithmetic
2.	spatial	extension	geometry
3.	kinematic	motion	dynamics, kinematics
4.	physical	energy	physics
5.	biotic	life	biology
6.	psychic (sensitive)	feeling	psychology
7.	analytic (logical)	distinction	logic
8.	historical	cultural development	history

9.	lingual	symbolic meaning	linguistics
10.	social	social interaction	sociology
11.	economic	profit, frugality	economics
12.	esthetic	harmony	esthetics
13.	juridical	retribution	legal studies
14.	moral	goodness, love	ethics
15.	fiduciary (pistic)	faith, ultimate meaning	theology

Dooyeweerd suggested that the higher aspects assume the lower aspects without being reducible to them. Thus, for example, movement (3) is only possible when there is space, but is, at the same time, something more and substantially different from spatiality. Of course, one can endlessly discuss whether, for example, the social aspect should be placed above the lingual, or vice versa (or whether both should share a place). Or one can ask whether there are really fifteen aspects and not fourteen or sixteen. Likewise, one can discuss whether the meaning nucleus of a particular aspect captures the essence of that aspect. For example, "retribution" seems to capture only part of the juridical function, and other ways of assigning legal parties their due (e.g., through restoration, as in the movement that aims at "restorative justice") should probably be included. While Dooyeweerd felt that the principle of aspects was more important than the number and place of the aspects, these kinds of questions have nevertheless been discussed vigorously among those in Dooyeweerd's school.

What is especially important in this philosophy, however, is that all these aspects have, so to speak, equal status. Thus, you do not do justice to reality when you suggest that it can be fully explained using physical (4) or biological (5) laws or explanations. Not everything can be exhaustively understood physically (4) or evolutionarily (5)—in fact, all things ("entities") have more aspects that are relevant to their being and functioning. Because the higher aspects are built on the lower ones, so to speak, they at the same time transcend them. In language that Karl Marx used (but contrary to what he said): the "superstructure" (in his case religion and faith) cannot simply be reduced to the "substructure" (the economy) but has its own proper place and function. Human beings are not just what they eat, as Marx's companion, Ludwig Feuerbach stated; people are defined just as well, and, presumably, even more so, by what they believe. And, to mention yet another example, moral awareness (14) is as real as mathematical knowledge (1 and 2).

Especially for scholars such a picture is very helpful, for it helps them to relativize their own discipline. That is difficult for everyone (a carpenter sees a hammer and a nail in everything; a merchant sees trade everywhere; a psychologist tends to explain everything psychologically; and a theologian can overestimate the role of faith), but according to Dooyeweerd you get stuck sooner or later if you absolutize one aspect. For reality itself resists such absolutization. Interestingly, this also applies to the highest aspect, the pistic one (after the Greek word for faith). This aspect too should not be absolutized, but neither should it be explained away by reducing it to some of the lower aspects. Of course, religious faith presupposes many things, such as moral awareness, a social group (usually one becomes a believer through contact with others), a certain cultural development, and even the functioning of psychological and biological processes. For example, no one can pray without certain processes in the brain functioning properly. However, that does not mean that faith can be reduced entirely to such processes, or that your faith is "nothing but" the result of social processes (such as the way you have been raised). Also, faith is undeniably related to psychological characteristics, such as the ability to surrender oneself in trust, as well as to feelings like joy and fear—but that does not mean that the only reason for your faith is that it counters your fears. Furthermore, this philosophy leaves room for numerous scholarly disciplines, each of which, using its own methodologies, studies one part of "the wisdom of God in its rich variety" (Eph 3:10). So, there can be a variety of scholarly contributions, and no one discipline is methodologically "the boss."

We give these short comments about this non-reductionist philosophy just to show that philosophy can be more than empty rhetoric and nice-sounding arguments, but that *good* philosophy can be a great help toward clear thinking. Thus, you do not have to go along uncritically with whatever ideas happen to be in vogue. Instead, the philosophy we have described briefly can help to keep the faith instead of carrying you away from it.

Questions for Discussion

1. How do you view the idea that an epistle presented as written by Paul (or Peter) may not be written by that apostle but actually by one or more of his students? Do you not have any problems with this (e.g.,

because of what was explained above about pseudepigraphy), or do you think that God would certainly not have allowed this to happen?

2. What do you think about the fact that we still don't know what some texts in the Bible are referring to? To what extent is that problematic for your faith? Why can we nevertheless speak (with the Reformers) about the "perspicuity (or clarity) of Scripture"?

3. Where and in what ways do you see the philosophy of scientism influence society? Discuss concrete examples of where and how science is absolutized or extolled and given too much authority.

4. Apart from the glorification of science we also see a lot of skepticism towards science today. The results of scientific research are then seen as "just an opinion." Which trend do you think is stronger? And which do you find more dangerous?

Group Activity

Think in advance about a situation in which you struggled or, better yet, struggle, with the relationship between your faith and certain scientific claims or a scientific theory.

Step 1. Tell in three minutes what the problem is and which tension you felt or experience. The others do not interrupt you.

Step 2. Now the group members take turns asking you a question on the basis of what you have told them. All questions are valid, even the ones that seem silly at first sight. You write down all the questions.

Step 3. You answer the questions, shortly and to the point.

Step 4. The others now discuss the situation as if you weren't there. They discuss what the real problem is and how you could deal with it. You listen to their advice.

Step 5. You give a short reaction about the discussion and the advice, telling the group which insights you find helpful and which you don't (yet).

Then it's someone else's turn and you make a similar round as a group.

10

Test All Things

THE HEART OF SCHOLARLY work is research. Doing research is very popular today. Students in all the kinds of postsecondary institutions already begin with this during their studies. Some specifically indicate that they "want to go into research." It's a good discussion starter at a birthday party. Many different kinds of research continue to be possible—and useful! At the same time, some people continue to speak of their skepticism towards research and its (purported) outcomes. An elder in my church told me that he always harbored some suspicions when a message begins with "Research has shown that . . ." He had noticed how easily research data can be presented in such a way that it reflects the opinion of the researcher or the funder of the research more than the bare facts. However, in 1 Thessalonians 5:21, Paul seems to press the readers to do research. "Test all things," he even writes—his advice can hardly be broader! Now Paul is obviously not speaking about scientific research. But the attitude he conveys can nevertheless teach us some things in our reflections on faith and science.

Read: 1 Thessalonians 5:12–28

Testing Divine Providence?

In the opening scene of *The Bridge of San Luis Rey* (1927), the novel with which the American author Thornton Wilder won the Pulitzer Prize, the Franciscan monk, Brother Juniper, wants to give theology a place among the exact sciences. He had been looking for a way to do that for quite some time. However, he still lacked a laboratory, so to speak, until an opportunity is thrown into his lap as if by chance. On a warm day in July, 1714, he sees, at a completely random moment, that the suspension bridge of San Luis Rey, near Lima, collapses. Brother Juniper witnesses how the five people that were on the bridge make a deadly fall into the ravine below. The moment of the collapse of the bridge could not have been predicted and no one was responsible for it. Thus, it must have been an act of God. Therefore, this accident provided an opportunity for a "reliable test" of the doctrine of God's providence. If that doctrine is correct, then, so Brother Juniper thinks, it must be possible to trace why God allowed precisely these five people to perish in the collapse of the bridge. There must have been good reasons for that—and the whole novel then revolves around the question of whether such reasons can be discerned in the life histories of the five victims. An interesting plot!

The Role of Testing in the Faith

Brother Juniper was looking for a very important aspect of scholarly investigations: for the possibility of *testing* certain claims. He had gotten the impression that such testing was much more difficult in theology than in the "hard sciences." Indeed, that is often still seen to be the case. A major disadvantage of religious statements, it is often thought, is that they, unlike scientific statements, are not testable—and that they are therefore, so the idea goes, a stab in the dark. The question is, however, whether this difference is so black and white. Is testing in the sciences really so self-evident and unambiguous? And is it really so impossible in faith and theology?

To begin with the latter, testing is of great importance when it comes to faith and theology. In any case, that is what Paul is saying to the church in Thessalonica. When he has come to the end of his first letter to the Thessalonians, he gives a number of brief and succinct instructions that are intended to guide the life of the Christian congregation in Thessalonica into the right channels. In the first place, they deal with the relationship between leaders ("office bearers") and congregation members (vv. 12–13a), and then also with the mutual relationships between the congregation members (vv. 13b–15). Finally, a few clusters of exhortations for all individual church members follow in staccato style (was Paul's roll of papyrus running out?). Right now, we are particularly concerned with the last of these clusters:

Do not quench the Spirit.
Do not despise the words of prophets.
Test everything, hold fast to what is good.
Abstain from every form of evil.

While the King James Version translates verse 21a as "prove all things," most modern translations render the text as "test all things." The testing of all things that Paul calls for here has the character of considering or examining them and assessing their value.

What needs to be tested is described as "everything," but it is clear from the context that Paul is first thinking here of all the aforementioned prophecies. With this he wasn't thinking of the books of Isaiah, Jeremiah, and other prophets, but of specific messages that congregation members passed on to each other as being words from God, arising from each person's own situation. Apparently, there were people who wanted to silence such prophecies—possibly because it wasn't always clear that such words actually came from God. Paul doesn't agree with these critics, however. In any case, he tells his readers not to extinguish the Spirit, and he immediately connects this with "the words of prophets" that should not be despised. In other places too, it is clear that Paul sees prophecy as an important gift of the Holy Spirit (1 Cor 14). The Spirit is like a fire that can warm and excite you in all kinds of ways (Acts 2:2). But apparently you can put out that fire by closing yourself off to the gifts of the Spirit and by quenching or extinguishing the Spirit. At the same time Paul realizes well that, when it comes to this, it's not only gold that glitters. For surely, it is always tempting to take for a message of God's Spirit something that actually comes out of one's own mind! So we can understand that Paul calls his readers to be discerning: test (consider) all things—such prophecies, to begin with—and hold on to what is good. With what is good, he must have intended those insights that actually come from God. On the other hand, you have to avoid the things that come from a different source. It is remarkable that in many congregations and churches new interest has arisen in prophecy, in the sense that it is discussed here, and that even now the request for reliable testing is emerging again.

How did Paul visualize the testing that is referred to here? He does not mention that. From other New Testament texts we know, however, that prophecies must be saturated with the realization that in Jesus Christ, God himself came to earth in order to save the world. In 1 John 4:1–3 believers are called not to trust every spirit, but to "test [same word] the spirits to see whether they are from God." Here, too, a connection is made to prophecy: "for many false prophets have gone out into the world." But every spirit or prophecy that acknowledges that Jesus Christ has assumed human existence is from God. In other words, the incarnation, the becoming a human being of God's Son, is the touchstone par excellence. Christians are sometimes portrayed as naïve or gullible, but their faith actually makes them critical instead. The Greek verb *krino*, the root of critical, literally means to distinguish. In the Christian faith we are indeed challenged to distinguish between what is good and what is not good. To determine that, there is an important criterion: examine how a particular prophet or movement thinks about Jesus. Today, too, that remains a measuring stick that is of great importance, for example, in discerning whether populist leaders who claim to stand in the (Judeo)Christian tradition can be trusted or not: how do they actually think about Jesus, about his origin, his teachings (e.g., his Sermon on the Mount), and his suffering, death, and resurrection?

Testing in Academic Research

One could say that this critical, testing-based approach contributed to the fertile ground upon which the sciences could eventually start to grow. More generally, the Christian faith has been quite conducive to the rise of modern science. To be sure, other religious and philosophical traditions have also contributed to its emergence—it's actually quite a complex story how modern science came on the scene in the seventeenth century. Yet, it is very well conceivable that Paul's admonition to test all things made an impact alongside all sorts of other factors. In any case, all contemporary scientific disciplines stand or fall with thorough testing procedures. The heart of scientific knowledge production is research, we saw above. We can now add that the heart of doing research is testing things. The importance of that was shown, once again, when in 2020 and 2021 good vaccines had to be developed against the coronavirus. Only by testing potential vaccines before they were to be used for all people could it be established which vaccines did or did not work well.

Testing in the various scientific disciplines is not always a simple thing. Throughout the centuries it has become clear that it is not so difficult to come up with a certain theory, but it is more difficult to test that theory in an acceptable way. Philosophers of science have given much thought and spent much time discussing how this testing can and should be done.

In this they mainly focused on the natural sciences because here testing procedures seemed to be quite clear and straightforward. But even there, good testing turned out to be more complicated than was first thought. We follow their search for a moment (of course in a highly simplified form, and with the omission of countless details). We do so because in this way it immediately becomes clear how this relates to the testing of theories in the sphere of faith. In the first half of the twentieth century, philosophers of science thought that you could only take seriously those theories that had been proven (or "verified") with absolute certainty. Thus, for any claim to be meaningful and true, the test of verification should be passed: the claim should be *proven*. It soon became apparent, however, that his criterion was much too strict; we hold all kinds of things to be true that we cannot prove. Even the "verification theory" itself cannot be proven. Nor can, strictly speaking, natural laws be proven. For example, a law, such as "all iron rods expand when heated" cannot be proven, because it is impossible to actually heat all iron rods and then observe whether they expand. Real robust proofs seem to only be possible in mathematics.

That is why at some point the demands for proof were scaled back a bit. It would be sufficient if a certain theory would be *confirmed* by repeated observations. That seemed to be reasonable. If you observe often enough that iron rods expand upon heating, then, at some point (though it is difficult to say when that should be), you may conclude that they always do so under the same conditions. But even this adjustment turned out to be extremely problematic. It was particularly the well-known philosopher of science Karl Popper (1902–1994), whom we also met in the first Bible study, who pointed this out. He became so famous for this that he is one of the few thinkers that is routinely mentioned somewhere in almost any academic program. In 1919, as a teenager, Popper volunteered in a Viennese clinic for difficult-to-raise children, which was led by the famous psychologist Alfred Adler. He noticed at that time that Adler was able to reduce all the problems that these young people had to an inferiority complex that continued to affect them. No matter what behaviors these children exhibited, Adler knew how to twist the evidence in such a way that it all confirmed the theory that he himself had formulated. At the same time, Popper noticed that someone like Albert Einstein theorized in exactly the opposite manner; he indicated under which circumstances his theory of relativity would *not* be correct. Thus, he looked for a possible refutation of it. He indicated, for example, that if light from the stars passing the sun would not be bent to some degree, his theory would be refuted. That could only be checked during a solar eclipse—and, lo and behold, Einstein turned out to be right.

In the search for possible refutations (or "falsifications") of a theory, Popper saw *the* way to assess a scientific theory. The more attempts of disproval a theory could withstand, the stronger its status became. But even if a theory had survived various attempts at refutation, there was always the possibility that it could fail at the next attempt. For example, eventually Einstein's prediction about starlight bending when it passed the sun—which was a test for his theory—turned out to be not entirely correct. Apparently, science does not progress because more and more theories are "proven," but because more and more theories are disproven. It steadily comes closer to the truth, but it can never say with certainty that it has reached it. This is too great a goal for testing to achieve. At the time, Popper's critique put a huge dent in the triumphalism that marked large segments of the scientific enterprise.

The Role of Paradigms

But things would get worse. For in practice, even after Popper, numerous researchers did not strive to refute their own theories but, instead, constantly and studiously worked to avoid falsification, and when problems for their theory did occur, they worked hard to control the damage as much as they could. Why did (and do) they do that? Because they usually had very good reasons. For the underlying basic theory that was the starting point of their departure into new research had so often proved to be sound that it would be strange to just set it aside in the event of one unexpected research result. In such a situation it is more reasonable to see if you can still find a way forward around the unexpected problem, so that the whole theory upon which the research is based does not collapse. And, yes, sometimes that takes some radical adjustments—no human efforts are foreign to scientists in this regard.

It was in particular the well-known physicist and philosopher of science Thomas Kuhn (1922–1996), who (following others, by the way) drew attention to the fact that theories are usually connected in complex ways into larger wholes. Such a greater network of theories, including presuppositions, assumptions on how you can test them, proper methods of working, etc., Kuhn called a *paradigm*. That word—we can no longer imagine doing without it—was coined by Kuhn. We have already encountered several such paradigms: heliocentrism, geocentrism, the Darwinian theory of evolution, and Einstein's theory of relativity. In such comprehensive frameworks of thought, all things hang together and are related to each other in intricate ways. Paradigms form a "conceptual framework" from which one looks at things. They often depend on deep-seated convictions, presuppositions, and expectations. They also raise numerous internal questions that can be compared to puzzles that need to be solved. That often succeeds well, and in that case we are dealing with "normal science."

At some times, however, certain persistent puzzles remain unsolved for a long time. Then, if a proposal from a particular scientist emerges to look for the solution of that puzzle in an entirely different direction, a clash may arise between the old and the proposed new "paradigm." That was the case, for example, when all kinds of astronomical phenomena became increasingly difficult to understand on the basis of the theory that the earth is at the center of our solar system, and Copernicus came up with the idea to approach it the other way around through the theory of heliocentrism. In such a situation (and that was indeed the case here) it can take a while before it becomes clear who is right. It is not a matter of simple testing! Rather, it requires a lot of insight to decide whether or not to let go of a huge arsenal of beliefs and arguments with which you have grown up.

Indeed, a paradigm is like a house in which you have been raised and where everything is in a familiar place. Therefore, a move, or even a revolution (the word is Kuhn's), is needed to change from the old to the new paradigm. When you take that step, practically nothing stays the same because you start to look at things in an entirely new way. Scientists often do that only after vigorous resistance (not unlike some believers, such as C. S. Lewis, who unwillingly come to the faith). That is, if they do so at all, for as the physicist Max Planck said, science advances one funeral at a time: many scientists cling to untenable paradigms until their death. Only after their death do their students dare to put these old views to rest.

The point now is that *within* one and the same paradigm all kinds of theories can be tested, or, at least, it is clear under what conditions that could be done. However, what is much more difficult, if not impossible, is testing a paradigm itself. Everyone finds themselves ensconced in such a comprehensive theoretical framework and looks at the world from there. Your paradigm even determines to a large extent what you consider to be rational. So there is no objective point of view from which you can weigh paradigms against each other. For this reason, there are hardly any "neutral" standards that can be used to test them. There are a few—such as the simplicity, scope, and precision of a theory—but these are so general that they are usually not applicable. Only slowly but surely, as experimental evidence accumulates, can it become clear which paradigm will ultimately win the day. Fortunately, most scientists do not lose any sleep over this, because they are thoroughly convinced about the paradigm in which they work and because that paradigm has no major competitors. That does not alter the fact that in their everyday activities there are certain assumptions and values that play a major role and that are usually not discussed.

Paradigms in the Faith

It's remarkable that testing in the realm of faith takes place in more or less the same way as it does in science. When Paul calls for prophecies—prophecies can be compared to theories—to be tested, he is referring to testing *from within* the paradigm of faith. For the criterion, as we saw, is whether such prophecies recognize Jesus as the Son of God. But whether this criterion is itself correct—that is, whether Jesus is actually the Son of God—is no longer an item to be tested. On the one hand, that is because it is not clear how such testing could be done. But, on the other hand, it is because Paul is so deeply convinced of the gospel, particularly through his encounter with the risen Christ, that he has no doubts about this.

Paul's certainty was, so to speak, of a basic nature, and was not a derived (reasoned) certainty. He had become a Christian because he had been personally touched by the gospel, and not through some impersonal testing procedure. In short, what a paradigm is for a scientist—a deep-seated set of fundamental assumptions that have impressed you and have become convincing to you because of what it made you "see"—is the Christian faith for the believer. As C. S. Lewis (to refer to him once more) put it: coming to the faith is not like starting to look into the sun, but starting to see everything in the light of the sun. And just as you cannot test a paradigm in any easy way—for it's much too comprehensive for that—you also cannot test your fundamental faith assumptions. For it is impossible to position yourself outside all your beliefs about life in order to compare, from a sort of Archimedean point, the pros and cons and then draw the only possible conclusion. In fact, you are personally and deeply involved in things from the very beginning, in the same way that scientists are very personally, at times even dogmatically, involved in the "school of thought" that they work in.

An interesting example of what can happen when your "paradigm of faith" no longer works well and you end up in a crisis is illustrated in the well-known Gospel story of the two disciples walking to Emmaus (Luke 24:13–35). These two people had a deeply rooted, specific image of what they expected the Messiah to be. That image was badly shaken when Jesus died a shameful death, which happened against all their expectations. But then Jesus himself showed them that the Scriptures, on which they thought their image of the Messiah was based, should be interpreted very differently. Then all the pieces of the puzzle fell spontaneously into place and everything suddenly made sense. When the people from Emmaus then recognize the living Lord himself in the breaking of the bread (v. 30–31; did they see his wounds?), they are definitively changed and their conversion is a fact. It's as if they are stepping into a new life. From then on, nothing will be the same. Since then, the Christian faith has become a *new* way of looking at things for millions of other people, a way which turned out to be much more convincing since it did more justice to the totality of their experiences than all kinds of old paradigms.

Once Again: Brother Juniper

It is important to have a clear understanding of this striking similarity between faith and science. For it means that testing, in both cases, including in science, is by no means a simple thing. Testing in the hard sciences is not an easy thing and it is even less so in the "softer" social sciences and the humanities. Nevertheless, testing in all scholarly disciplines is indeed needed, but mainly within existing paradigms, and hardly, or not at all, between paradigms. In the same way, the Christian faith as a whole cannot simply be tested in comparison with other religions or views of life, as if a clear outcome could then result. Rather, it asks for a commitment that is founded on having been deeply and experientially touched by Jesus Christ himself. He made the life-changing challenge to love the Lord God "with all your heart, and with all your soul, and with all your mind, and with all your strength" (Mark 12:30). Thus, our mind does not take an insignificant place here, but not the primary one either.

In short, it is not the case that statements in the natural sciences are testable and theological ones are not, so that the latter are left up in the air. Brother Juniper could have saved himself the trouble of a search for a theology that was as "hard" as the exact sciences, because from a paradigm perspective in the end there is not such a big difference between the two. What does hold true is that in the natural sciences there are (fortunately!) considerably fewer paradigms than in the world of faith and theology, so that in the former we can agree more quickly and more often on all kinds of things. The fact that there is much less consensus when it comes to views of life is partly due to the fact that these are about such encompassing and elusive things: about the meaning of life, for example, about who we are as human beings, and about the nature and purpose of the reality in which we live. But theology is especially about a God who, in his majesty, by definition, is not subject to our observations and measurements. He reveals himself whenever he wills and to whom he wills. You are blessed when you have entered the house of the Christian faith, no matter how that happened, and when you have seen the pieces of your life's puzzle fall into place. In that case you come to stand in the world with your eyes wide open and you indeed try to examine and test all things you encounter on life's journey in order to preserve the good that is in it.

Questions for Discussion

1. This chapter begins with an example from the world of literature. Discuss the connection between literature studies and faith. Modern literature is often associated with the erosion and breakdown of faith. Can literature also call forth or strengthen faith? If so, what is needed for that to occur?

2. "Do not quench the Spirit," Paul writes. That would also mean that you may be a Christian with enthusiasm, passion, and emotion. Is that more difficult for people with a studious or rational-scientific bent than for others? Or doesn't it make any difference?

3. Just as the other disciplines, theology aims to make testable statements. But how could statements of faith be tested, do you think? Or is that not needed at all because faith simply transcends reason? In this context, how do you see the role of theology? Do theologians perform a useful task, are they dangerous because they put the faith in the same category as the sciences, or do you see them in an even different way?

4. One of the most visible outcomes of modern science is the advanced *technology* that is pervasive in modern society. Our modern

technological devices and gadgets have profoundly transformed our way of life in many ways (especially in the West). Are these modern technologies a blessing or a curse in your opinion? If it can be both ways, how do you test this and "hold fast to what is good" while abstaining from what is evil?

Group Activity

In keeping with the theme of this Bible study, here is a short test to see whether you, as a group, experience the things that are discussed in this chapter in the same way or differently. After each statement indicate which answer fits best with your opinion. Then compare your answers with those of the others and explain to each other why you have put a mark in the relevant place.

Decision: Definite No   —   —   Certainly

1. Faith in Jesus as the Son of God who became human is still the best touchstone for deciding who may be considered to be a Christian.

   ☐ — ☐ — ☐ — ☐

2. The Christian faith can be disproved by future research.

   ☐ — ☐ — ☐ — ☐

3. In terms of testability, the Christian faith is quite similar to a scientific paradigm.

   ☐ — ☐ — ☐ — ☐

4. In science there will always remain a certain measure of uncertainty, and in faith that is exactly the same.

   ☐ — ☐ — ☐ — ☐

5. The paradigm theory of Thomas Kuhn does not do enough justice to the fact that science supports its theories with hard facts.

   ☐ — ☐ — ☐ — ☐

6. When someone says, "research has shown that . . ." you always have to be suspicious.

☐ — ☐ — ☐ — ☐

7. Taking notice of the history of science helps to relativize the claims of science.

☐ — ☐ — ☐ — ☐

8. A Christian is a critical person.

☐ — ☐ — ☐ — ☐

Some Literature

Here are some suggestions for those (e.g., Bible study group leaders) who want to expand their grasp on the main themes of the preceding chapters.

General

Ian G. Barbour, *Religion and Science: Historical and Contemporary Issues* (New York: HarperCollins, 1997).

Francis S. Collins, *The Language of God: A Scientist Presents Evidence for Belief* (New York: Free Press, 2006).

Cees Dekker, Corien Oranje, and Gijsbert van den Brink, *Dawn: A Proton's Tale of Everything that Came to Be* (Downers Grove, IL: IVP, 2021).

Alister E. McGrath, *The Foundations of Dialogue in Science and Religion* (Malden, MA: Blackwell, 1999).

History

John Hedley Brooke, *Science and Religion: Some Historical Perspectives* (Cambridge: Cambridge University Press, 1991/2014).

Peter Harrison, *The Territories of Science and Religion* (Chicago: The University of Chicago Press, 2015).

Reijer Hooykaas, *Religion and the Rise of Modern Science* (Grand Rapids: Eerdmans, 1972).

Ronald L. Numbers, ed., *Galileo Goes to Jail and Other Myths about Science and Religion* (Cambridge: Harvard University Press, 2009).

Evolutionary Biology

Denis Alexander, *Creation or Evolution: Do We Have to Choose?*, 2nd ed. (Oxford: Lion Hudson, 2014).

Some Literature

Deborah B. Haarsma and Loren D. Haarsma, *Origins: Christian Perspectives on Creation, Evolution, and Intelligent Design*, rev. ed. (Grand Rapids: Faith Alive, 2011).

Denis O. Lamoureux, *I Love Jesus and I Accept Evolution* (Eugene, OR: Wipf & Stock, 2009).

Gijsbert van den Brink, *Reformed Theology and Evolutionary Theory* (Grand Rapids: Eerdmans, 2020).

The Natural Sciences

Rodney Holder, *God, the Multiverse, and Everything: Modern Cosmology and the Argument from Design* (Aldershot: Ashgate, 2004).

Jeffrey Koperski, *Divine Action, Determinism, and the Laws of Nature* (New York: Routledge, 2021).

Del Ratzsch, *Science and Its Limits. The Natural Sciences in Christian Perspective* (Downers Grove, IL: InterVarsity, 2000).

Philosophy

Roy Clouser, *The Myth of Religious Neutrality. As Essay on the Hidden Role of Religious Belief in Theory*, rev. ed. (Notre Dame: University of Notre Dame Press, 2005).

Alvin Plantinga, *Where the Conflict Really Lies: Science, Religion, and Naturalism* (Oxford: Oxford University Press, 2011).

Mikael Stenmark, *Scientism: Science, Ethics, and Religion* (Aldershot: Ashgate, 2001).

Nicholas Wolterstorff, *Reason within the Bounds of Religion*, 2nd ed. (Grand Rapids: Eerdmans, 1984).

Theology

Geoffrey H. Fulkerson and Joel Thomas Chopp, eds., *Science and the Doctrine of Creation* (Downers Grove, IL: InterVarsity, 2021).

John Polkinghorne, *Science and Theology: An Introduction* (Minneapolis: Fortress, 1998).

Gijsbert van den Brink, *Philosophy of Science for Theologians: An Introduction* (Frankfurt: Peter Lang, 2009).

Genesis 1–11

C. John Collins, *Reading Genesis Well: Navigating History, Poetry, Science, and Truth in Genesis 1–11* (Grand Rapids: Zondervan, 2018).

William Lane Craig, *In Quest of the Historical Adam* (Grand Rapids: Eerdmans, 2021).

John H. Walton, *The Lost World of Adam and Eve: Genesis 2–3 and the Human Origins Debate* (Downers Grove, IL: InterVarsity, 2015).

Handbooks

Paul Copan et al., eds., *Dictionary of Christianity and Science* (Grand Rapids: Zondervan, 2017).

John P. Slattery, ed., *T&T Clark Handbook of Christian Theology and the Modern Sciences* (London: T&T Clark, 2020).

J. B. Stump and Alan G. Padgett, eds., *The Blackwell Companion to Science and Christianity* (Chichester: Blackwell, 2012).

Scripture Index

Italicized verses correspond to chapters on these passages